# brief history of
# paradigm
# shifts
# in christian education

## VIC WIENS
### BRE, BEd, MEd

FriesenPress

One Printers Way
Altona, MB R0G 0B0
Canada

www.friesenpress.com

ISBN
978-1-03-912364-9 (Hardcover)
978-1-03-912363-2 (Paperback)
978-1-03-912365-6 (eBook)

*1. RELIGION, CHRISTIAN EDUCATION, CHILDREN & YOUTH*

Distributed to the trade by The Ingram Book Company

# Table of Contents

# Introduction

It all became very real to me as I held my baby daughter for the first time. Although I had been involved in the Christian education of other parents' children and youth in churches, camps, and Christian schools for many years, it all took on a whole new meaning as I looked into my baby daughter's eyes.

The mandate for God's people to pass on their Judeo-Christian faith to the next generation has been well understood for thousands of years. The first explicit command is found in Deuteronomy 6:1–7, where Moses instructed the Israelite fathers as follows:

> These are the commands, decrees, and laws the Lord your God directed me to teach you to observe in the land that you are crossing the Jordan to possess, so that you, your children, and their children after them may fear the Lord your God as long as you live by keeping all his decrees and commandments that I give you, and so that you may enjoy long life .... Impress them on your children. Talk about them when you sit at home and when you walk along the road, when you lie down and when you get up (New International Version).

At some point in our lives, however, it is important that this becomes personal. This brief history of the application of these Bible passages to different cultural realities reflects my own personal journey of discovering how God's people have passed on their faith in different cultural contexts.

As we will see throughout this book, the way in which God's people have fulfilled this and many other similar injunctions has varied significantly through changes in cultures and economies. Sometimes the changes in methodology have been very gradual and

> This book is designed to help pastors, parents, and workers in Christian education understand the historical context of Christian education, to identify changes that have already happened in our new cultural and economic paradigm, and to gain historical perspective as they discern the further changes that will likely need to happen in the near future.

at other times the changes have been rapid. Given the rapid cultural and economic changes that we are experiencing at this time in history, our methodologies for instructing our children are also changing rapidly. This book is designed to help pastors, parents, and workers in Christian education understand the historical context of Christian education, to identify changes that have already happened in our new cultural and economic paradigm, and to gain historical perspective as they discern the further changes that will likely need to happen in the near future. A planned sequel to this book will delve deeper into effective Christian education strategies for this new paradigm.

Christians in every age have needed to discern how to live out their part in God's continuing story. As Scot McKnight so aptly stated in his book, *The Blue Parakeet,*

> First, we need to be mastered by the *Story* by reading the Bible so deeply that its story becomes our story. If we let that story become our story, we will inhabit the Bible's own story .... Second, together as God's people we are to *discern* how to live in our world. Our calling is to live out the ageless Story in our world. To do this we have to bring back the Spirit of God into our interpretation of the Bible. We read the Bible with all the tools of history

and language that we can muster, but a proper reading
of the Bible is attended by the Spirit, who will trans-
form us, guide us, and give us discernment to know
how to live in our world (McKnight, p. 212).

I have personally been involved in virtually every facet of Christian
education for my whole life, as a learner, as a helper, as a teacher, and
as a leader. My first degree is a Bachelor of Religious Education from
a Christian college. From there I continued my training and invested
most of my career to work as a teacher, administrator, and consultant in
private Christian schools, obtaining both a B.Ed. degree and an M. Ed
degree. In addition to these degree programs, I continued taking courses
that focused on various aspects of Christian education, so that I have the
equivalent of eleven years of postsecondary education related to Christian
education. Throughout this time, I served in various capacities in local
churches' Christian education programs in several church denominations. I say this not in a boastful way but to say that I have been, and
continue to be, a student of education in general and of Christian education in particular.

I am now a grandfather, and as I hold each new grandchild, I relive
that moment when I first felt the very personal responsibility of passing
on my faith to my daughter. I am also still involved in formal Christian
education leadership and consulting, and I need to understand how to
pass on the Christian faith in our rapidly changing Western culture.

Fifty years ago, while I was still in high school, a good friend introduced me to church history, and especially to the writings of the early
church fathers. Around the same time, I was introduced to a writer in
my own denomination, Delbert Wiens (no relation), who had written an
article titled "New Wineskins for Old Wine." In this article, the writer
explored how we needed to rethink the discipleship of the children of
disciples. In particular, he challenged our Anabaptist denomination to
develop a theology of nurture. This challenged me to find out what the
early church fathers taught about the nurture of the children of disciples
in their era. I was surprized by how significant a role Christian education

3

played in evangelism and the discipleship of children in the early church. I have continued to study this theme for these subsequent fifty years. Through this study, I developed personal approaches to Christian education for children coming from adult baptism denominations as well as those coming from infant baptism denominations. Since all of the private Christian schools I worked in were interdenominational, this was an immensely helpful foundation for my work as a teacher, administrator, and consultant.

In September 2006, when I had completed my work as senior administrator with one particular Christian school, I spent significant time in prayer seeking God's guidance for my next kingdom assignment, given some significant health problems. That month our pastor preached a sermon series titled "Shift ... New Wine, New Wineskins." Given the influence of the earlier article on new wineskins, I certainly resonated with the sermon series. In the middle of one of these sermons, God clearly spoke to me, saying, "You will no longer work in Christian schools in the old paradigm, but you will again serve in Christian schools in the new paradigm."

Since I had never heard about a new paradigm in Christian schools, I began to research this phrase. To my surprise, I found several Internet articles about a new paradigm in Christian school education and about the new paradigm in secular education. I also found information on changes to various church based weekend, after school, and evening forms of Christian education. For the last fifteen years I have continued to research various facets of this new paradigm in Christian education and have tried to discern how God would have us approach this facet of discipleship in a way that is consistent with scripture and the ongoing story of God and his people.

A few years later, I joined the staff leadership team at my local church, and I began to assess this new paradigm in Christian education for children and youth through a church ministry lens. During this time, I wrote an article for our church leadership team titled "Discipling the Children of Disciples," which looked at the various historical approaches to the education of children and youth used by God's people, beginning with the patriarchs and ending in our own recent era. My research for this article opened my eyes to a much richer history of Christian education than I had been exposed to in my Bachelor of Christian Education program at Bible college or my training as a Christian school educator, and this book is an expansion of that article.

My work since that time has largely been in several aspects of that new paradigm in Christian education. However, I feel like I have just been nibbling at the edges of this new paradigm in my work as a Christian education leader and consultant. Recently, I felt a strong conviction that it was time to move the dialogue about the new Christian education paradigm to another level, and this book is a first step in that direction.

The goal of this book is not that readers adopt all of the ideas presented, but rather that we study the history of Judeo-Christian education, as well as our current cultural paradigm shift, and discern how our churches and Christian schools should adapt to remain culturally relevant yet biblically grounded. In other words, let's rethink how the church needs to disciple the children and youth of disciples in this new cultural paradigm, as well as bring new people to faith through Christian education. I trust that this book will catalyze such discussions and actions.

# What Are Paradigm Shifts?

## 250-Year Paradigm Shifts

In 2017, we celebrated the five-hundred-year anniversary of the Protestant Reformation. The Reformation is a good example of what a paradigm shift looks

> The very term, postmodernism, only explains that modernism is on its way out, and we really don't know yet just what will replace it.

like. A number of historians have identified a 250-year revolution cycle. The 250-year revolution cycle is typically the product of technology disruptions that are accompanied by social disruptions. In our generation, that technology is the digitization of knowledge, and the social disruption is the emergence of postmodernism, which may only be the transition to a yet-to-be identified culture. While economists study these cycles in order to anticipate investment opportunities and risks, we need to study them in order to anticipate Christian education opportunities and risks.

We also need to understand why these times of paradigm change are called revolutions. While the early adopters of change are pushing for change, the slower adopters of change can make life exceedingly difficult for the early adopters. However, the agents of change always win in these transitions, even if they have to pay for the wins with their very lives. Progress itself is more constant than the revolution terminology suggests, but how people think about their culture does change more rapidly during paradigm shifts.

The modernism paradigm is only about 250 years old, and yet the new postmodern trend has already reached a tipping point so that modernism is on its way out. The very term, postmodernism, only explains that modernism is on its way out, and we really don't know yet just what will replace it. Various scholars are proposing terms like post-postmodernism and metamodernism to describe the new culture, but none of these terms have really caught on because the new culture is not yet fully developed. What we can see is that we are in a significant paradigm shift that is as big as the shift to modernism, and postmodernism is only part of this revolution.

Some writers, such as Phyllis Tickle, combine two of these 250-year cycles into one 500-year cycle, but the concepts are much the same. In fact, I recommend Phyllis Tickle's book, *The Great Emergence*, which looks at paradigm shifts within church history. Some researchers have also tried to make a strong case that these cycles are actually caused by weather, as they seem to parallel periods of warm weather and periods of cold weather. Whatever the cause, we can see from history that significant positive and negative cultural changes happen in roughly 250-year segments, and that we are currently in one of the transition points. We are in a major paradigm shift.

## The Protestant Revolution and the Capitalist Revolution

What many people do not understand is that the Reformation was part of a much larger socioeconomic paradigm shift in western Europe. The Reformation was both a natural outcome of, and yet a repudiation of, the Renaissance, which is how we generally label the previous paradigm. In particular, the Reformation was a continuation of the culture of reform of the Renaissance. As De Lamar Jensen wrote in his book, *Reformation Europe,*

> The Renaissance was an age of reformers. They wanted
> to reform education, correct the errors of medieval
> scholarship, improve the translations of legal and

religious texts, enrich the content as well as the style of
literature, recover the wisdom of the ancient, recapture
the order and simplicity of nature, and renew and refine
the relationship between man and God by thoroughly
reforming the church. (p.3)

On the other hand, the Reformation was also a repudiation of the
Italian Renaissance. Many Europeans viewed the Roman Catholic
Church as corrupt and as having become even more corrupt through the
Renaissance. Martin Luther's Ninety-five Theses was aimed at the moral
corruption of the church as much as its theological corruption. The
tension between what Rodney Stark calls the "Church of Power" and the
"Church of Piety" in his book *How the West Won* was not new to Europe,
because it was not uncommon since the time of the Roman emperor,
Constantine. During the Reformation era, the Pope belonged to the
Church of Power, while Martin Luther and most of the other reformers
belonged to the Church of Piety. What changed was the willingness and
ability of the reformers to solicit enough support from local governments
to obtain protection. Otherwise, Martin Luther would simply have been
another martyr.

While it is well-known that several city-states in Italy played a significant role in the development of capitalism, it is not so widely known
that the Church of Piety, led by monks in their monasteries, also played
a significant role in the development of capitalism, which is another
feature of the Reformation era. Monasteries were often the recipients of
land donations, and monks worked the land to provide funds for their
own support as well as their charitable acts. Over time, monastic orders
purchased additional land to accommodate their growing populations,
and even purchased land for outposts of their orders. Initially, monasteries simply produced what they consumed themselves. Then monasteries
began specializing in their production, selling what they didn't need,
and purchasing what they did not produce themselves. Many monasteries also grew into towns as various shops and trades were set up to
supply those commodities the monasteries did not produce themselves.

As monasteries grew into complex organizations, they also developed managerial skills. Because monks lived simple lives, the monasteries soon accumulated wealth and became lenders. Their wealth also allowed monasteries to hire workers in order to further expand production.

Both the spread of capitalism and the belief in the virtue of work became part of the "Protestant work ethic" of the Protestant Reformation and even the Catholic Counter-Reformation. It is not that capitalism, or the work ethic, were new in this era, but rather that they became in vogue. That is the nature of paradigm shifts.

Technology also played an important role in the Reformation. Civil wars had become more devastating with the development of several technological advances in warfare. Gunpowder, and the subsequent use of cannons, became common in Europe by about 1350 AD. Guns became common by 1500 AD, creating a whole new class of soldier, the infantryman. Guns significantly increased the loss of life in the constant wars in Europe. Death by war and disease created a preoccupation with death that is evident in both art and literature in that era.

Technology also allowed ideas to spread significantly faster. Johannes Gutenberg had improved printing by developing a method for mass producing movable type, and with this improvement, a wide variety of pamphlets and manuscripts began to spread around Europe. As a result, more people had a desire to learn to read and also to think for themselves about various ideas. By the mid-1450s, Gutenberg had printed Latin Bibles, allowing many more people to read and interpret the Bible for themselves. Printing presses also allowed Luther to print and sell many of his German Bibles so that people could read them for themselves.

The Reformation also coincided with the age of exploration. While the Portuguese had already found their way around the tip of Africa to begin trade with India, it was Columbus's accidental discovery of the New World in 1492 that significantly reshaped Europeans' view of their world.

Economic changes were happening at the same time. Feudalism was breaking down on account of the rise of capitalism and the shortage of labor caused by the Black Death, and many peasants became free to pursue work off their farms. Many peasants became poor farm workers and earned just enough for themselves and their families to stay alive. Other peasants were able to become sharecroppers or leaseholders. While sharecroppers had a hard time improving their economic situation, leaseholders were often able to improve their lots economically by implementing various agricultural improvements, such as buying animals and tools, and by improving the land.

Other peasants found their ways into the cities, which were growing rapidly. Although many peasants became poor day laborers in the cities as well, others were able to get into trades or open up shops. Merchants became a new power group as money, rather than land, became the key currency. As city populations grew, so did the demand for food, providing farmers with a source of money as well. Wool for clothing also became a valuable farm commodity, and banking increased in importance. The Reformation, which was primarily a religious revolution, coincided with the capitalist revolution.

I encourage everyone who wants to understand both the economic progress of this time and what was happening in Christendom in Europe leading up to the Reformation to read Rodney Stark's book *How the West Won*. This book corrects many misconceptions most people have of both the religious and economic context of the Reformation era.

## The Industrial Revolution and Modernism

The Industrial Revolution, which happened roughly 250 years later, was part of a larger social paradigm shift that also precipitated the French Revolution and the American Revolution. All of these revolutions coincided with what is often referred to as Modernism and the Scottish Enlightenment.

While paradigm shifts are often thought of as discontinuities, they are perhaps better thought of as the logical progression, even if very rapid, of previous paradigms. The Reformation was, in many ways, the logical progression from the Italian Renaissance, which had begun almost 250 years before. Likewise, the Scottish Enlightenment was, in many ways, a logical progression from the Reformation.

It was John Knox who had brought John Calvin's version of the Reformation to Scotland, and he gave it a unique twist that ultimately led to the Scottish Enlightenment. Knox was able to persuade the Scottish nobles to do away with all physical manifestations of Roman Catholicism in the Scottish Lowlands and replace it with the Scottish Kirk. The Scottish Kirk was a harsh institution that banned almost all forms of communal fun from the culture. For example, the Kirk banned Carnival, Maytime celebrations, Passion plays, gambling, dancing, card playing, and the theater, as well as any form of work or play on Sundays. The Kirk enforced its prohibitions with severe physical punishments.

On the other hand, the Scots were expected to learn to read the Bible on their own. Over time, John Knox's vision of having a school in every parish became a reality, and over a few hundred years Scotland developed the highest literacy rate in the world, thought to have been around 75 percent by the time of the Scottish Enlightenment.

Knox also strongly opposed the power of Scotland's monarchs. It didn't help matters that the monarchs he dealt with in his lifetime were either children or women, neither of which fit his idea of a suitable leader. Knox and his close allies taught that God had ordained political power to belong to the people, not to monarchs or nobles. One of Knox's closest allies, George Buchanan, published a book on *The Law of Kingship Among the Scots* in 1579. In this book, he articulated the belief that the people were always more powerful than their rulers and that the people were free and sometimes obligated to remove their leaders if they failed to act in the people's interests. Even within the Kirk, ministers were chosen by the congregation's elders, not by political or church rulers. Church leaders at the highest level were chosen by the Kirk's General Assembly, which consisted of local church representatives.

While various monarchs tried to push back against the power of the Kirk and of the Scottish people, they never succeeded because the people resisted so vehemently. For example, in 1638, the people signed the National Covenant in droves, declaring their determination to uphold the Kirk and the power of the people in the face of forced Anglicization. Some people even signed the Covenant in their own blood, and the Covenanters raised an army that successfully resisted the king's imposition of power and attempts at Anglicization of the Kirk.

However, Scottish Calvinism also had its downside, and it was the reaction to the negatives that ultimately led to the Scottish Enlightenment. While the Kirk strongly advocated for the power of the people as a whole, it did not allow for much individual freedom of thought and speech. Yet the literacy rate was high in order to enable every person to read the Bible, creating an audience for books. By about 1750, almost every town had developed a lending library so that even the poorest people had access to a wide variety of both religious and secular books. It was this high rate of literacy and the market for books, together with a desire for greater intellectual freedom, that eventually led to the Scottish Enlightenment and Modernism.

> It was this high rate of literacy and the market for books, together with a desire for greater intellectual freedom, that eventually led to the Scottish Enlightenment and Modernism.

Just as important as the high literacy rate was the role of Scottish universities. Both Glasgow and St. Andrews universities had already been established in the Middle Ages, but they became more accessible as the literacy rate increased. Several new universities were also established. Scottish universities also enacted low tuition fees that were only about 10 percent of the cost of attending Oxford or Cambridge in England.

The Scottish Enlightenment and Modernism grew out of these Scottish universities. As Arthur Herman says it in *How the Scots Invented the Modern World*,

> The Scottish Enlightenment is the intellectual movement that laid the foundation for how all of us think about ourselves in relation to the modern world. Almost

everything that shapes the way we think about society, politics, science, culture, and history flows from the pens of a small group of men who lived in Edinburgh, Glasgow, and Aberdeen, in the mid-18ᵗʰ century.

A number of French thinkers were also significant contributors to the Enlightenment, and in many respects, they had already laid the foundation for the Scottish Enlightenment. In particular, René Descartes laid the foundation for beginning with reason rather than scripture as the basis of knowledge. French and Scottish thinkers read each other's work and built on each other's ideas.

The Christian faith, as well as Christian schools as we know them today, were deeply influenced by modernism. While some Christians embraced modernism, others reacted to it and yet were unknowingly significantly influenced by it.

At its root, modernism elevated human reasoning and rational scientific thinking, and a significant percentage of the modern authors, were Scottish. These include:

- Adam Smith: *Wealth of Nations*, which still sets the tone for many economics courses
- David Hume: *Treatise of Human Nature* and *Essays Political, Literary and Moral*
- Adam Ferguson: *Essay on the History of Civil Society*
- Thomas Reid: *Inquiry into the Human Mind*
- Francis Hutcheson: *System of Moral Philosophy* and *An Inquiry into the Origin of Our Ideas of Beauty and Virtue*
- Lord Kames: *Sketches of the History of Man*

These and other figures of what has become known as the Scottish Enlightenment essentially reordered human knowledge. They sought to bring the principles of human reasoning and the rational scientific method into every area of knowledge, including religion.

As in all paradigm shifts, this was not exactly new thinking. The Scholastic thinkers had already applied reasoning to theology and science for many centuries, and they were the ones who had developed the scientific method. However, the Scottish Enlightenment increasingly severed scientific thinking from its Christian context. To the Scholastic thinkers, science was a subset of theology, as they thought more in terms of special revelation and general revelation, with science being part of general revelation. I think it is fair to say that the Scholastic thinkers viewed reason through the lens of religion, while the Enlightenment thinkers viewed religion through the lens of reason.

The Industrial Revolution was in many ways a product of the Scottish Enlightenment, even though there had already been significant industrial innovation before the Enlightenment. So was the American Revolution, which produced, in many ways, the first modern nation based on the principles of modernism advocated by the authors of the Scottish Enlightenment. The French Revolution soon followed.

Over time, modernism was embraced by thinkers throughout what has become known as the Western world. As a result, the Enlightenment became much more than the Scottish Enlightenment, and modernism is a name we use to identify Enlightenment thinking.

Modernism deeply impacted the Christian faith in the Western world, both directly and indirectly. Directly, modernism influenced people to rely less on the authority of their various church bodies and caused many people to leave their traditional Christian beliefs. Indirectly, through movements such as the Great Awakening, it led to a focus on the individual, with an emphasis on personal faith. It caused many people who had left their faith during the Enlightenment to return to their faith in a more personal and experiential way. In other ways, however, the Great Awakening was a reaction to the heavy focus on reason. The Great Awakening drew heavily on people's emotions. Together, these movements challenged people to think and act individually and determine on their own what was best for them personally rather than just accept what was handed down to them from government or religious authorities.

Prior to the Enlightenment, education was almost exclusively the domain of churches, or at least church denominations. In other words, most schools in the Western world were parochial Christian schools. In some communities, however, various church groups had already created joint interdenominational Christian schools.

Horace Mann, who lived in Massachusetts in the USA, is often credited with being the founder of the secular public school system in the 1820s and 1830s. He did not believe that any religious doctrine should be taught in publicly funded schools, which were primarily elementary schools at that time. The few secondary schools and schools of higher education remained in the hands of churches and Christian organizations for the time being. Other states and countries in the Western world followed Horace Mann's example, and this profoundly changed Christian education throughout the westernized world. Over time, secular public education also took over much of secondary and postsecondary education throughout the westernized world. This secular education largely followed the philosophies articulated by the Enlightenment.

However, there were several church bodies that held fast to Christian school education. In the USA, for example, Roman Catholics, Lutherans, Dutch Calvinists, Mennonites, the Amish, and Moravians continued to operate their own Christian schools in many areas. By the close of World War II, many Christian families, especially in the USA and Canada, became genuinely concerned with the secular education their children were receiving in public schools. The 1962 and 1963 US Supreme Court rulings disallowing public prayer and Bible reading in public schools became the impetus for the most recent Christian school movement. We will take a closer look at this movement, which in hindsight developed during the transition from the Modern era to the Postmodern era. Then we will turn to what appears to be happening as the new postmodern era is becoming the dominant paradigm.

> The 1962 and 1963 US Supreme Court rulings disallowing public prayer and Bible reading in public schools became the impetus for the most recent Christian school movement.

## The Knowledge Revolution and the
## Transition to Postmodernism

Historians generally believe that we are currently experiencing another paradigm shift of this significant 250-year magnitude, based on a shift from modernism to postmodernism and from an industrial economy to a knowledge-based artificial intelligence economy. It is important to understand that any term that begins with "post" does not really define the new thing, but rather indicates that the old has gone. While several names have been suggested to define this new era, not one of them has stuck to date, so we continue to use the term postmodernism.

Historically, World War II was a significant turning point from the Enlightenment (modernism) to postmodernism. One of the powerful driving forces of modernism was the metanarrative of progress based on reason. While this was not a new thought from the Enlightenment, prior to the Enlightenment, progress was always tied to the religious belief that the world was moving toward a more complete expression of God's kingdom. Now the concept of progress was being separated from religious belief and simply being founded on reason.

World War I was originally called the Great War, and it was thought to end all wars. Therefore, World War II came as a huge disappointment to modern thinkers. A number of countries also committed themselves to providing funds for postsecondary education for war veterans, resulting in a significant increase in the education levels in these countries. Writing shortly after WWII, Peter Drucker, the well-known economics author, suggested that the transition to "a yet nameless" postmodern world was happening as he was writing his 1957 book, *Landmarks of Tomorrow*. In his view, it consisted of a shift from reason and mechanical cause to pattern, purpose, and process. In his view, according to Wikipedia, the key elements of this postmodern culture were "the emergence of an Educated Society, the importance of international development, the decline of the nation state, and the collapse of the viability of non-Western cultures."

More recently, postmodernism has been identified with relativism and pluralism in many aspects of culture. It is in many respects just the logical conclusion of modernism, which did away with objective faith and morals. For sure, the word "truth" no longer has the same meaning as it did prior to this new era. We will explore postmodernism more fully in later chapters of this book.

The post WWII Christian school and homeschool movements have been a reaction to this new relativistic and pluralistic culture. However, to a large extent, the recent Christian school movement sought to go back to "the good old days" rather than accept the inevitability of the new cultural paradigm and become truly relevant to it.

## Fifty- to Sixty-Year Paradigm Shifts

A number of shorter and longer term social and economic trends within these larger paradigms are also contributing to the current paradigm shift in Christian education.

Jack Lessinger, for example, has charted the fifty-to-sixty-year economic shifts in the USA, which have been mirrored in Canada as well. These economic shifts have reflected lesser but still important cultural shifts. Lessinger terms the ending era of consumerism the "Little King" and the emerging era "Responsible Capitalism." His research and recent book, *The Great Prosperity of 2020*, suggest that we are currently nearing the end of a time of transition and that Responsible Capitalism will have "won" the transition within a few years.

I believe that the dramatic political shift in Alberta and Canada, where I live, over the last few years reflects this smaller cultural shift as much as it reflects the larger postmodern shift. Responsible Capitalism includes environmental concern, human rights, and many other social concerns. This is a sharp contrast to the heavy focus on the consumer. While we have been resisting the excesses of consumerism in Christian education in our generation, the new generation will have to resist the excesses of social responsibility. We already see this in gender-related issues. As

Lessinger's diagrams indicate we are likely to see responsible capitalism as the dominant paradigm in education for the next thirty years or so.

However, the most significant cultural shifts that affect Christian education are the larger 250-year cultural revolutions. If we combine the shift to postmodernism with the shift to responsible capitalism, we have the essence of the current cultural paradigm that Christian schools find themselves in.

## Generational Shifts

Generational shifts are not paradigm shifts, but they are still worth mentioning in this context, because they also require a retooling of Christian education. These generational shifts occur about every fifteen years. I am personally part of the baby boomer

> Generational shifts are not paradigm shifts, but they are still worth mentioning in this context, because they also require a retooling of Christian education.

generation, born roughly between 1946 and 1964. Generation X was born roughly between 1965 and 1979, while the millennial generation was born roughly between 1980 and 1994. iGen (or Gen Z) refers to the generation that was born beginning in 1995 and their end date is still hard to define, but it is thought to end around 2012 or 2015. The latest generation, born after 2012 or 2015 and sometimes called Generation Alpha, is still too young to define as of this writing, although books such as *Generation Alpha*, by Mark McCrindle, make a good attempt. While these generational shifts are not as pronounced as paradigm shifts, they still require some retooling of Christian education.

# How Have God's People Adapted in Paradigm Shifts?

## Paradigm Shifts in Bible Times and Church History

God's people encountered paradigm shifts in Bible times as well. Both the expression of faith and the faith-based education of God's people, even before the time of Jesus Christ, historically changed with paradigm shifts in culture. There are both opportunities and risks associated with

God's people encountered paradigm shifts in Bible times as well. Both the expression of faith and the faith-based education of God's people, even before the time of Jesus Christ, historically changed with paradigm shifts in culture.

such shifts in the expression of faith. Christian leaders typically look back to the early church as they reinvent the church in a new paradigm, and this is a healthy exercise. However, Christians are also prone to adopt elements of the new culture into the Church without serious evaluation, and this leads to unhealthy syncretism. Paradigm shifts, like the Reformation, allow us to re-evaluate our Christian traditions and toss out those that do not fit the new culture as well as those that have actually allowed error to creep into the Church. During these paradigm shifts in faith, we must be careful to not introduce new errors into the Church.

Christian education that takes place in Christian homes, as well as the Christian education programs of churches and of Christian schools inevitably reflects current church culture, but these aspects of Christian education also have a significant ability to shape church culture in times of paradigm change as they teach future Christian leaders. This means that Christian education leaders and workers need to be especially mindful of paradigm shifts in faith and need to be leaders in translating the Christian faith into the new cultural paradigms.

I grew up learning dispensational theology, which taught that God dealt with his people in unique ways in different eras throughout biblical history. As I studied the Bible and various other theological viewpoints, I concluded that dispensational theology was only partially correct. While dispensational theology rightly identified various ways in which God dealt with his people, these dispensational theologians, such as John Darby and Cyrus I. Scofield, missed the connection between the different eras and the different cultural contexts within which God's people lived. Each so-called dispensation was actually a distinct cultural context that required new modes of worship and practices.

## Egyptian Paradigm

Abraham is the first clear example of a God follower adapting to a new culture. Abraham and Sarah grew up in Ur of the Chaldees. My impression from studying the cultures of the Middle East at the time of Abraham is that Ur and its area of cultural influence was the most advanced culture of its time, but that Egypt was rising up as next the new superculture. There were many wealthy people in Ur, and the "Common District" was filled with schools, libraries, markets, as well as some very impressive homes with lush gardens. Abraham appears to have been one of these wealthy people, although it is not clear whether he actually lived in the city. Abraham's first move was to Haran, which was still within the cultural and economic sphere of Ur, as maps of that time period show.

When Abraham finally moved to Canaan, he left the Chaldean culture and moved into the Egyptian culture. While we think of Canaan as being quite separate from Egypt, at times it was part of the Egyptian

Empire, while at other times it was part of the Egyptian socioeconomic sphere but outside of the actual Egyptian Empire, in much the same way that Canada is part of the American socioeconomic sphere. The most vivid example of a shift in faith practice that came with this move to another culture is the rite of male circumcision. Male circumcision appears to have been a purification rite in ancient Egypt, so it would have made sense in that culture that God's holy nation would adopt male circumcision. In fact, God gave Abraham clear direction in this regard.

Contemporary missionaries are quite accustomed to translating the Christian faith into different cultures. I find the most accurate explanations of this process to come from authors who personally experienced Christian missions. While it is certainly true that many missionaries tried to westernize their converts, many missionaries also sought to translate the Christian faith into indigenous cultures. I recently read Lamin Sanneh's books, *Translating the Message: The Missionary Impact on Culture* and *Disciples of All Nations: Pillars of World Christianity.* Sanneh was born to an ancient African royal family in Gambia, in western Africa. He grew up as a Muslim and converted to Christianity in his teenage years. While he agrees that missionaries came to Africa with mixed motives, he asserts that their willingness to translate the Christian message and scriptures into indigenous languages also served to translate the faith into indigenous cultures. Sanneh contends that the Christian faith can be expressed in any language and interpreted in any culture, and that this feature of Christianity has helped it continue to spread to new cultures. He asserted that indigenous cultures benefited from the Christian faith. Coming from an African Muslim background, Sanneh demonstrates that translatability is a characteristic mode of Christian expansion, whereas cultural diffusion, that is the lack of translation, is a more characteristic mode of Muslim expansion.

We need to take on this same missionary translation mindset as we transition the Christian

> We need to take on this same missionary translation mindset as we transition the Christian faith into a new culture in our own westernized countries.

faith into a new culture in our own westernized countries. In every cultural context, the church also needs to ensure that it has an effective process for discipling children of disciples. With every cultural transition, God's people have indeed historically changed the way in which their children were taught.

In the days of the patriarchs and later of the Israelite clans, teaching was done primarily by fathers and grandfathers. This was consistent with their culture. Abram (later called Abraham), for example, was still part of his father's household while in Ur and Haran. When he left Haran, he became the head of his own household. The household was the basic family and economic unit during this era. Abram had a large household even before he had his own children. In Genesis 12, God told Abram to "Leave your country and your father's household and go to the land I will show you..." (v. 1). He traveled to Canaan with "... his wife Sarai, his nephew Lot, all the possessions they had accumulated and the people they had acquired in Haran ..." (v. 5). When Lot was captured by enemy kings along with the people of his city, Abram "... called out the 318 trained men born in his household and went in pursuit ..." (v. 14). Abram's fighting force from within his own household was powerful enough to conquer the enemy kings and rescue Lot and the other captives, as well as all their captured possessions. Isaac inherited not only all Abraham's possessions but his whole household.

God even clarified for Abraham who was to be included in his household when he was given instructions on circumcision, which we find recorded in Genesis 17:12:

> For the generations to come every male among you who
> is eight days old must be circumcised, including those
> born in your household or bought with money from a
> foreigner—those who are not your offspring.

This instruction makes it truly clear that the household included both family members and servants, and that Abraham was effectively making the faith decision on behalf of his entire household. This was the cultural norm in his era.

This household system was still firmly in place when Joshua told the Israelites, "But for me and my household, we will serve the Lord" (Josh. 24:15). In those days, patriarchs decided on behalf of their whole families which religion they would adopt. There was no individual choice in that culture, even in ancient Israel. Likewise, it was the patriarch's responsibility to teach his whole household the ways of God. Most patriarchs had two to four adult sons, their son's children, and often their son's grandchildren living in close proximity to them. It was also common for households to have aged mothers living within them. It was common for wealthier households to include debt servants, slaves, concubines, resident aliens, and day laborers. Patriarchs were responsible to oversee the religious education of this whole household.

Until quite recently, it was common for children to begin doing work on family farms and in family businesses from a young age. Then, at around age twelve to fourteen, they began what we could call apprenticeships under their own extended family, or sometimes under some other farmer or business owner. The transfer of faith continued through this apprenticeship phase. If youth performed their apprenticeship with another family, they became part of that household. Girls were often married at around age fourteen, and the young married couples were generally part of larger households, where the young men and women continued to receive guidance from the patriarchs and their wives.

It is common for homeschooling families to use the family context of education in the patriarch era as the basis for teaching their children at home. While this is not an inaccurate interpretation

> Religious education in a household would more likely have included twenty to thirty children than four children.

of these Old Testament passages, it is an incomplete interpretation. Religious education in a household would more likely have included twenty to thirty children than four children. A more complete view of household education in our culture would be homeschooling led by the oldest surviving male in an extended family, his wife, and children, as well as any grandchildren and great-grandchildren. It would also include all employees of family-owned businesses, their children, and grandchildren, as well as any single mothers and their children who are living with this family. As you can see, this is a vastly different picture than our current small homeschool arrangements.

After the Mosaic law was given, priests and Levites also played an important role in religious education. Both were instructed to teach the people the commands God had given them. However, there is no indication that priests and Levites taught children in that era. That responsibility appears to have remained with household patriarchs and their adult sons.

In the kingdom period, the kings set up schools for their households as well. These royal households were sometimes exceptionally large. We know, for example, from I Kings 4, that King Solomon's household consumed vast amounts of food every day. We also know that his household included seven hundred wives of royal birth as well as three hundred concubines. We can only imagine how

> Solomon had twelve district governors over all Israel, who supplied provisions for the king and the royal household....
>
> Solomon's daily provisions were thirty cors of the finest flour and sixty cors of meal, ten head of stall-fed cattle, twenty pasture-fed cattle and a hundred sheep and goats, as well as deer, gazelles, roebucks and choice fowl.
>
> I Kings 4: 7, 22–23

many children and servants were also part of his household. Even if only the male sons of his wives attended King Solomon's school, there could have been three hundred to five hundred students in this household school at any given time. We know that the Book of Proverbs was one of Solomon's textbooks for his school, along with Moses's law. Many of the teachers in the kings' schools were sages, or scholars as we would refer to them in our culture.

The kings' schools most likely also included children of key royal administrators. The language of Daniel 1:3–4 indicates that Daniel and his friends were students in the kings' school of their day. There it says that King Nebuchadnezzar ordered his chief court official to "… bring in some of the Israelites from the royal family and the nobility—young men without any physical defect, handsome, showing aptitude for every kind of learning, well informed, quick to understand, and qualified to serve in the king's palace." This gives us a good picture of the kind of students the king's school in Jerusalem produced at the time of the exile.

There is no indication in the Bible or other historical sources that the common people attended schools led by scholars in Israel or Judah in the kingdom era. From what I can tell, the household education and the apprenticeship model continued for the common people during this time, since I have been unable to find any sources referring to a new model in this era.

The only other schools during the nation period mentioned in the Bible are the schools of the prophets. These schools of the prophets are mentioned several times during this nation period. For example, in I Samuel 19, we see Samuel leading a group of prophets, though it is hard to tell whether he is instructing them as well. In II Kings 2, we read that Elisha meets the "company of prophets" in Bethel and they prophesy that God will take Elijah from him that day. This prophetic word is repeated by another company of prophets in Jericho and then again at the Jordan River by a third company of prophets. After Elijah is taken up by the chariot of fire, fifty prophets from Jericho go looking for Elijah for three days. In II Kings 4, we find Elisha meeting with a company of prophets in Gilgal. While there is no mention of these groups of prophets being schools, we do know that they were following leaders in an era when apprenticeship was a primary mode of career preparation. It is likely that youth began their prophetic apprenticeships at the usual age of around twelve to fourteen years.

While Israel and Judah were influenced by many of the surrounding cultures, the Egyptian culture continued as the dominant culture until the exile.

## Persian Paradigm

While the northern Kingdom of Israel was dispersed into the Assyrian Empire well before the exile of Judea, we have few records of their continuation of faith-based education. Many of the true God followers in Israel had already moved or fled to Judea before or around the time of the dispersion of the northern kingdom. From this time on, we talk about the Jews as one people group, even though the population of Judea included many people from the northern Israelite tribes. It is this combined group of Jews that were taken into exile to Babylon, ending the independent nation of Judea and forcibly transitioning the Jews into a new cultural paradigm.

The Babylonian exile and the destruction of the temple in Jerusalem produced the Jewish synagogue form of worship and teaching. Jewish historians sometimes assert that the synagogue predates the exile in some form, but the synagogue as a central component of Jewish worship and teaching was more likely a product of the Babylonian exile after the temple in Jerusalem was destroyed around 586 BC.

> The Babylonian exile and the destruction of the temple in Jerusalem produced the Jewish synagogue form of worship and teaching.

We know from II Kings 24:15–16 that King Nebuchadnezzar exiled the most capable people of Judea. This passage states that:

> He also took from Jerusalem to Babylon the king's mother, his wives, his officials, and the leading men of the land. The king of Babylon also deported to Babylon the entire force of seven thousand fighting men, strong and fit for war, and a thousand craftsmen and artisans.

When Judea again rebelled against Babylonian rule shortly after, the few remaining leaders were also taken to Babylon or fled to Egypt. There is good evidence for Jewish synagogues arising in both of these locations, although their dates of establishment are not as clear.

The Jews had either been living under Babylonian rule or in Egypt for only a few generations when the Babylonian and Egyptian empires were absorbed into the Persian Empire. Consequently, most of the era from the exile to the Greek period was under Persian rule in both Babylon and Egypt.

There is less evidence of synagogues being built by the remaining poor people in Judea prior to the return from exile and the building of the new temple under Ezra. However, synagogues began to play a significant role in Jewish education, both in Judea and in the Diaspora of Jews who were spread around the Middle East from around the time of Ezra. Historians tell us that within a short time, there apparently were more than one hundred synagogues across Palestine. Where numbers were not sufficient to build a separate synagogue building, Jews would meet in private homes for the same purpose. It appears that both instruction by patriarchs and the apprenticeship model also continued in this era.

The Protestant Old Testament story ends with the Jews living within the Persian Empire, and Judea as a province of that empire. The Book of Malachi, the last book to be written before the intertestamental period, was likely written about 430 BC. Judea remained within the Persian Empire for roughly another one hundred years, until 333 BC, when Alexander the Great conquered the Persian Empire.

The Protestant Bible focuses more attention on Jews living in Palestine during the Persian rule, so we rely more on other Jewish writings such as the deuterocanonical books, which are accepted as scripture by Catholics, and the pseudepigraphal writings, which are not considered scripture by either Protestants or Catholics, to understand how the Jews lived in Babylon, Egypt, and other parts of the Persian Empire as well as the later Greek empires. Economically, life was better for the Jews in Babylon and Egypt than in Palestine once they got settled. Eventually, some of the

Jews also resettled in other cities, especially after the Persians absorbed the Babylonian Empire.

While the center of Jewish faith was definitely the new temple in Jerusalem after seventy years of exile, it appears that outside of Jerusalem, the synagogues became increasingly important in the daily and weekly lives of the faithful. In particular, they became centers of religious education. Synagogue schools became the dominant form of Jewish education in this Persian period both in Judea and in other parts of the Persian Empire.

## Greek Paradigm

As Protestants, we know extraordinarily little about the intertestamental period because we do not read the books of the Apocrypha, or the deuterocanonical or intertestamental books, as they are known to Catholics. Anyone who reads the deuterocanonical books (Protestant Apocrypha), and especially I and II Maccabees, has a much better understanding of this intertestamental period.

In the intertestamental period, the Jews, both in Palestine and in the Diaspora, came under Greek rule as Alexander the Great expanded his empire. Within a short period of time, before his death at age thirty-two, Alexander had not only conquered significant territory but had also created seventy Greek cities across his vast empire and started the process of Hellenization, that is the process of making the Greek culture the dominant culture in his empire. According to tradition, Alexander was welcomed into Jerusalem by the Jews and shown from the Book of Daniel that his empire had been prophesied in advance. As a result, Alexander apparently granted the Jews a higher level of autonomy to exercise their religion than he was accustomed to giving to other religions within his empire.

When Alexander met his untimely death a few years later, his empire was divided into three smaller Greek empires. From 323 BC to 195 BC, Judea was part of the Egyptian Greek Empire, ruled by the Ptolemy dynasty. The Ptolemies allowed the Jews to continue their religious life much as it had been within the Persian Empire. Although there had been a gradual transition to Greek culture during that time, it was not forced on the Jews in Judea. Part of this transition seems to have included a higher level of participation in education.

Around 195 BC, the Syrian Greek Empire, ruled by the Seleucid dynasty, took Judea away from the Egyptian Greek Empire and began an era of forced Hellenization, including desecration of the temple in Jerusalem. The tension was intensified when some Jewish leaders offered to aid with this Hellenization in order to obtain favors from their ruler. Within a few years, the Seleucid rulers had built a Greek gymnasium, a center of Greek education and athletics, in Jerusalem. Apparently, it became common for Jewish boys to attend their Jewish synagogue schools in the morning and attend the Greek athletic training in the Greek gymnasium in the afternoons. This practice may have gained the acceptance of the Jewish leaders, even though athletes always practiced and performed naked, had the Greeks not insisted that the circumcised penis was immodest. As a result, many of the Jewish boys had their circumcision reversed by covering their circumcision with sheepskin, breaking the Mosaic law.

> Apparently, it became common for Jewish boys to attend their Jewish synagogue schools in the morning and attend the Greek athletic training in the Greek gymnasium in the afternoons.

The devout Jews became outraged and successfully revolted under the leadership of the Maccabees to become an independent nation. They remained relatively independent politically from 167 BC to 63 BC, when the Romans conquered them. The devout Maccabees

> The devout Maccabees determined to have all Jews educated in the Law of Moses and began to push for Jewish synagogue education for all children. By 75 BC, Jewish synagogue education was compulsory for children throughout the Maccabean Empire. Within a short time, there were 480 synagogue schools in the vicinity of Jerusalem.

determined to have all Jews educated in the Law of Moses and began to push for Jewish synagogue education for all children. By 75 BC, Jewish synagogue education was compulsory for children throughout the Maccabean Empire. Within a short time, there were 480 synagogue schools in the vicinity of Jerusalem.

It appears that the typical synagogue school building was a room, called a Beth Hassepher, or House of the Book, attached to the main synagogue building. Here both boys and, according to some historians, girls six to ten years of age were taught to read and write and were instructed in the Mosaic law as well as the mathematics needed to accurately calculate the tithe and conduct business. Following the Greek model, school began at sunrise for six days of the week. Less intense lessons even took place on the Sabbath. Only Jewish boys continued their education past age ten, with smaller cohorts progressing to each subsequent level of education. This model of Jewish education was permitted to continue even when the Romans conquered Judea in 63 BC. It continued in the Roman era until the destruction of Jerusalem in 70 AD.

While Jewish education was not compulsory outside Judea, many Jewish synagogues throughout the Greek empires and later throughout the Roman Empire also provided for optional Jewish synagogue education following the Judean model. Following an earlier Judean model, where there were not enough people or funds to build a separate synagogue, people would meet in larger homes or the homes of teachers for the same purpose. Older students who aspired to become rabbis (teachers) were typically apprenticed by leading rabbis, and this process became known as discipleship, based on the Greek pattern. These rabbinical apprentices also had to learn a trade that they could fall back on for income, because rabbis were typically paid through voluntary gifts rather than wages.

Did the Jews have the equivalent of our Sunday morning Bible teaching programs for children? Yes, but in Judea these teaching times assumed that children were also attending the synagogue schools. This assumption was not likely made in the many synagogues that were scattered throughout the Roman Empire.

Before looking at the early church era, it is important to focus on Jews living outside Palestine prior to that era. First of all, by the time of Christ,

> While Jewish education was not compulsory outside Judea, many Jewish synagogues throughout the Greek empires and later throughout the Roman Empire also provided for optional Jewish synagogue education following the Judean model.

there are estimated to have been at least six million ethnic Jews scattered throughout the cities of the Roman Empire, compared to only about one million in Palestine. As we will see in the next section, many of these ethnic Jews were no longer practicing Jews. In particular, many of the boys and men were not circumcised and therefore could not consider themselves Jews. However, it appears that many of these ethnic Jews throughout the empire continued to attend Jewish synagogues and their Jewish schools. These Diaspora Jews used the Septuagint, the Greek translation of the Jewish scriptures, in worship and in education because they talked, read, and thought in Greek.

Even Palestine had many Hellenized Jews and God-fearers, and it is interesting to note that Nazareth, where Jesus grew up, was located only a short walking distance from the wealthy Greek city of Sepphoris. There is considerable speculation that when Joseph and Mary moved to Nazareth, Joseph would have commuted to work as a carpenter in Sepphoris, or at least produced wood products for Sepphoris, which was undergoing significant reconstruction exactly during that time period.

While Jesus was not called to minister to the Greeks, it is highly likely that he was familiar with Greek culture and quite possibly also spoke Greek himself. Many historians believe that Jesus would have been fluent in Hebrew, Aramaic, and Greek, and likely was somewhat conversant in Latin. Jews in and around

> It is interesting to note that Nazareth, where Jesus grew up, was located only a short walking distance from the wealthy Greek city of Sepphoris.

---

Sepphoris were considerably more Hellenized than the Jews in Judea, and this may well be a factor in the Jewish leaders' question of what good could come from Nazareth. I do not believe that it was by chance that Jesus grew up in the context of Hellenized Judaism of Galilee rather than in the less Hellenized Judaism of Judea. Jesus is the Greek name for Joshua, and it is not clear whether he was known by his Hebrew, Aramaic, or Greek name prior to the writing of the New Testament.

We do not know how much Jewish education Jesus received, but it appears that at the very least he would have attended a synagogue school. Some scholars believe that he was also likely discipled by a rabbi, but I think that is just conjecture. It is more likely that Jesus worked as a carpenter, following his father's trade, until he began his public ministry. On the other hand, Jesus was recognized by the people as a rabbi, so there may indeed be some basis for that conjecture that Jesus had been discipled under some unknown Jewish rabbi before his own public ministry and been a carpenter only insofar as all rabbis had to also have a trade to fall back on.

In the Jewish education model around the time of Jesus, all children were expected to know the Scriptures, but out of one thousand boys, only about:

- one hundred would attain readiness to study the Mishna, and out of that group
- ten would attain readiness to study the Talmud, and out of that group
- one would attain the mastery needed to become a master, or rabbi.

We also do not know what level of education Jesus's disciples had prior to following him, but likely they had received the basic synagogue education before entering their respective occupations. It was the general rabbinic practice for disciples to record key teachings of their masters, so it is safe to assume that Jesus's disciples did the same. We must also understand the word "disciple" to mean "apprentice." Consequently, it

34

was normal for Jesus' disciples to be sent out to perform the same kind of ministry as their rabbi.

## Roman Greek Paradigm

The Roman Empire absorbed the Greek empires only a few generations before Jesus Christ was born. Even though Rome had conquered the Greek empires, the culture of the eastern half of the Roman Empire remained very Greek in its culture. Consequently, the early church developed its traditions within that Roman Greek culture.

It is important to think of the early church, especially in the first twenty years, as a Messianic "denomination" within Judaism. It appears that children of these early Christian parents sent their children to Messianic Jewish synagogue schools. My reading of early church history and the writings of the early church fathers suggests that because of the smaller size of Christian congregations, both the congregations and the schools more frequently met in private homes, as was the Jewish practice for smaller congregations. Most likely, at least some of their youth would have been apprenticed or discipled as teachers as well, though not in the usual sense, because Jesus had instructed his disciples not to pursue such a designation.

Researchers are not sure when this Jewish practice spread to other Christian congregations outside Judea, but it appears that it certainly became the common practice by around 70 AD, when many Jewish Christians spread out from Judea to major centers around the Roman Empire as a result of the siege and destruction of Jerusalem by the Romans. From this time on, it appears that churches throughout the empire tended to follow the Jewish model so that Christian synagogues (churches) were started wherever there were Christian families, and Christian schools started if there were school-age children. However, because of the small size of most of these churches and schools, they appear to have met in the homes of wealthier members of the church community instead of in dedicated buildings. The schools also sometimes met in the homes of teachers. We should also understand that the apprentices were first called Christians in Antioch, according to Acts 11:26. Of course, these apprentices could have been of all ages, from about fourteen to old age.

If we think of what homeschooling looks like today in large families, but expand the concept to household schooling, we would be quite close to what early Christian education based on the small synagogue school model looked like in the early church. The content, however, would not have looked similar, since the Old Testament was the primary textbook. This should be our mental picture when we think of the primary discipleship model of "the children and youth of disciples" in the early church. Judging by the rapid growth of the early church, it was a highly effective discipleship strategy.

It appears that the church developed a catechism for new believers and children of believers early in its history. From my readings of numerous sources over the last five decades, I have concluded that the Jews of the Diaspora had already developed a form of religious instruction for proselytes and for children who had not attended synagogue schools in key elements of their faith prior to admitting them into full participation in their synagogues. The early church appears to have adapted and formalized this process for the Christian faith early on in its history.

While I have not found conclusive evidence for this, my impression is that Christian schools in the early church covered the entire content of the catechism, which we know was taught to new adult believers, in addition to extensively studying the Old Testament. When we think of classes for new believers, we usually think of six-to-eight-week, one night per week, programs covering the rudiments of the Christian faith. Based on early church writings such as the *Apostolic Tradition* and the *Apostolic Constitutions*, catechism classes for new adult believers in the early church often took place over a two-to-three-year time span, held at least weekly, but sometimes even nightly.

These catechism classes typically covered:

- a survey of the Scriptures, emphasizing the sweep of salvation
- the central doctrines of the Christian faith

- commentary on the totality of the Scriptures
- Christian ethics based on the two ways: the way leading to life and the way leading to death
  - deliverance ministry

In other words, Christian education for both adults and children was intense in the early church. From what I can glean on the topic of early church Christian education, all children who did not receive the contents of the catechism in Christian schools were required to take the same catechism classes as new adult believers before they became active members.

One important insight from recent research is that many more of the early Gentile Christians appear to have been God-fearers before becoming Christians than was previously thought. When we read the Gospels, we get the impression that Jews totally separated themselves from gentiles. While this was largely true of life in Palestine, it was not the case where Jews were scattered throughout the Greek and later the Roman Empires. These scattered Jews apparently often included gentiles, and especially the God-fearers of Jewish ethnic background, in their synagogue schools. It also appears that many of the God-fearers who became Christians in the early church grew up attending Jewish schools. This explains how a book such as Romans could be written to gentile Christians while assuming so much background knowledge of the Old Testament.

The God-fearers appear to have included the following kinds of people:

a. families where a Jewish girl had married a non-Jew, but the family remained attached to the synagogue worship and Jewish school
b. gentile members of Jewish "households," including hired men, maids, and slaves with their families
c. families from Jewish ethnic backgrounds who did not circumcise their boys so they could participate in Greek schools, sports, and careers but otherwise held on to their Jewish beliefs
d. gentile families with no direct Jewish connection, but who were attracted to the monotheism and high morality of the Jews and

who chose to worship in the synagogues and then decided to send
their children to Jewish schools

e. gentile families with no direct Jewish connection, but who
decided to send their children to Jewish schools because of the
Christians' love for children and their ability to develop moral
character, and then also began to join the synagogue worship.

When we understand the background and composition of the God-
fearers, it is easier to understand how so many gentile Christians were
very comfortable with discipling their children through Christian schools
that functioned so much like the Jewish schools.

It should be noted that, in particular, Christians were known for their
more equal love for girls, who were treated poorly by the pagans. As a
result, many converts to Christianity in the early church were girls and
women, and this appears to have been reflected in the composition of
students in Christian schools, at least among the younger students.
Consequently, non-Christian parents and newly converted parents who
sent their boys to pagan schools sometimes sent their daughters to
Christian schools.

On the other hand, it appears that among gentile Christians who
came from totally pagan backgrounds, not as many sent their children to
Christian schools, but rather many continued to send their boys to the free pagan schools. If they sent their girls to school at all, it was frequently to the Christian schools. While the early churches did require new converts to learn the catechism before becoming active members, I have not I have not found much evidence for the existence of strong alternative models of discipleship for these children and youth who did not attend Christian schools in the early church, other than the requirement for them to take the catechism classes later in life. This created a tension in the early church that is similar to the tension experienced in our culture between Christians who send their children to Christian schools or provide Christian homeschooling for their own children versus those who send their children to public schools.

found much evidence for the existence of strong alternative models of discipleship for these children and youth who did not attend Christian schools in the early church, other than the requirement for them to take the catechism classes later in life. This created a tension in the early church that is similar to the tension experienced in our culture between Christians who send their children to Christian schools or provide Christian homeschooling for their own children versus those who send their children to public schools.

The writings of early church fathers lead us to believe that this tension was not fully resolved by the time Constantine converted to Christianity. By then the Roman public schools were losing their popularity as government funding diminished and as Christians became the majority in the Roman Empire, so Christian schools more easily became the dominant model and pagan schools were eventually outlawed throughout the Roman Empire under Christian emperors.

## Roman Paradigm

Emperor Constantine brought significant changes to the Roman Empire's religious scene, and this had a significant impact on Christian education as well. Under Constantine, the church was more strongly influenced by Roman culture. While other emperors had already allowed for some degree of religious freedom in the Roman Empire, Constantine was the first emperor to convert to Christianity. Although he granted religious freedom to almost all religions, he granted special favor to Christianity after the Edict of Milan in 313 AD. However, he also involved himself in church politics and influenced the future direction of the church.

By the end of Constantine's reign as emperor, Christian teachers had begun to occupy positions in previously pagan schools, and by the end of that century, Christians had become leaders in Roman education at all levels. Through their

> Through their influence, Christian teachers gradually Christianized the classical education system of the empire.

influence, Christian teachers gradually Christianized the classical education system of the empire. This was a significant change from the earlier era when the profession of classical schoolteacher was grounds for being disqualified from Christian baptism. At the same time, Christian schools became more willing to include aspects of classical education into their program of studies.

Before that century ended, in 391 AD, Emperor Theodosius had issued a decree making pagan worship, including that in pagan classical schools, illegal. In many ways, St. Augustine's books, such as *The City of God* and *On Christian Doctrine,* completed the transition to incorporating the most valuable aspects of classical education into Christian education, at least in theory.

Constantine also altered the structure of the Roman Empire by relocating the central seat of governance from Rome to Constantinople (Byzantium) and solidifying the earlier division of the empire into the eastern (largely Greek) and western (largely Latin) administrative units. Consequently, when Rome fell to the barbarians in 476 AD, the empire came to be known as the Byzantine Empire, and its language of administration and culture was Greek. This Byzantine Empire continued for another one thousand years. It is in this setting that we begin to see Christian schools that blended Christian discipleship with strong academic teaching, developing into what is now often called Christian "classical education."

However, the barbarians maintained many of the administrative and educational structures in what had previously been the western half of the empire, and Latin remained the language of administration and culture. One of the key leaders of the Latin Christian classical education movement, Boethius, served in a key bureaucratic role under an Ostrogoth emperor. However, Christian classical education, using Latin as their language of instruction, developed mostly in monasteries and churches in the west after the barbarian takeover of the western half of the Roman Empire.

After St. Patrick brought Christianity to Ireland, this island became one of the most advanced Christian classical education centers in the fifth and sixth centuries AD. During this era, scholars from Ireland migrated to various parts of western Europe to teach classical Christian education, using Latin as their primary language of instruction. Ireland's culture was

> After St. Patrick brought Christianity to Ireland, this island became one of the most advanced Christian classical education centers in the fifth and sixth centuries AD.

so vibrant at this time that many authors suggest Ireland avoided what is often known as the Dark Ages in Europe.

## Viking Paradigm

As the western half of the Roman Empire began to disintegrate, various barbarian tribes began to coalesce. Many historians call this period the Dark Ages because of the decline in classical culture in what had been the western half of the Roman Empire.

In Gaul, over time the Frankish tribes joined forces to gain control of a large area in what is now mostly northern France. Charles Martel, known as The Hammer, gained control of this Frankish kingdom in 718 AD and expanded its boundaries. However, it is Charles Martel's grandson, Charlemagne, who is better known as the founder of the Holy Roman Empire. Although Charlemagne had already become king of the Franks in 768 AD, it was on Christmas Day in 800 AD that Pope Leo III crowned him as emperor of the Roman Empire. From that time, Charlemagne set out to revive the Christian Roman Empire in Europe. It was this relationship with the papacy that contributed to its significant influence on all of Europe.

Charlemagne's consolidation of much of western Europe under one administration brought a level of peace and economic prosperity this region had not experienced since the disintegration of the Western Roman Empire. This prosperity permitted significant building projects, resulting in hundreds of new buildings such as cathedrals, monasteries, and royal residences in less than one hundred years.

Since Latin was still the common language of politics and religion, Charlemagne was concerned with the lack of Latin literacy in his empire. In order to address this void, he attracted Latin-speaking scholars

> Charlemagne set up a number of schools and created a standardized curriculum based on the Christian classical education model.

from around Europe to his court until their Frankish students were able to rise to the same scholarly level and become teachers. Charlemagne set up a number of schools and created a standardized curriculum based on the Christian classical education model. He modernized Latin by developing a new form of script, the use of lowercase letters, and a system for adding new words while retaining the traditional Latin rules of grammar and phonics. During this "Carolingian Renaissance," as Charlemagne's era has come to be known, scholars produced over one hundred thousand manuscripts of classical works. Latin literacy contributed to a more educated government administration and also a more educated Christian priesthood throughout a significant part of Europe.

An overview of this time period is not complete without evaluating the impact of the Vikings. In fact, their influence was so dramatic that I have labeled this paradigm with their name. The Vikings began to raid Europe during the reign of Charlemagne and continued their exploits until around 1100 AD. It is not surprising that the Vikings appeared in what had been the Western Roman Empire at roughly the same time as Charlemagne. Europe was unstable, so opportunists took advantage.

Historians suggest that Vikings first began raiding to obtain plunder to enhance their status and for patronage because resources were limited within Viking home territory. The breakdown of the Roman Empire also significantly reduced trade, another previous source of Viking wealth. The Vikings buried valuables with their owners who had died, requiring a continuous supply of replacements.

However, during this time period, their primary motives for raiding appear to have been slaves and wives. The Vikings used slaves themselves, but they were also active slave traders. The Arabs and Byzantines purchased many slaves during these years, and the Vikings had no qualms about capturing and selling slaves. In their own communities, men prided themselves in having enough women and slaves to do all their work so they could spend all their time drinking and raiding. In Norway, it appears that in order for a young Viking man to begin his own farm, he would need to have obtained twelve cattle, two horses, and three slaves.

Young Viking men were also eager to obtain wives. It appears that raiding served the purpose of "collecting" silver, which was needed to pay the bride price required to marry local women. The Vikings practiced polygamy, and only wealthy men had the means to take all the available girls in their own communities. As a result, the other young men would engage in raids to obtain wives for themselves. Female slaves were often sex slaves in addition to being work slaves, and the children of these sex slaves also became slaves of their owners.

Of course, polygamy also results in population increase. Agricultural land was limited in most of Scandinavia, so a growth in population increased pressure on already limited available land. As a result, the Vikings increasingly turned to trading and became more urban. The slave trade just happened to be the most lucrative form of trade.

Charlemagne was not blind to the Viking threat. He responded by increasing the size of his navy. While it is easy to view the Viking threat only from the side of the Christian world, the Vikings were also afraid of Charlemagne. He was their biggest threat, as they could see from the brutal way in which he conquered the Saxon lands just to the south of Denmark. In addition, because of the political tension with Charlemagne, the Vikings were no longer eager to trade with their Saxon neighbors. When Charlemagne died, his empire became weak, and the Vikings saw this as an opportunity to raid more freely.

The word "slave" comes from the word Slav, since much of the Viking slave trade consisted of capturing Slavic people and selling them as slaves to the Byzantine and Muslim empires. The Vikings also raided Muslim lands. However, the Muslims were much more effective in their military responses than the weak Christian lands. The Muslim lands were much farther from the Viking homeland. The Vikings also attacked Constantinople but were unable to break through the city's massive wall.

Over time, many Vikings conquered land and settled down outside of Scandinavia and adopted the Christian faith. After years of constant Viking raids into the Holy Roman Empire, the Frankish king, Charles the Simple, signed a treaty with Viking leader Rollo, giving the Vikings a portion of Normandy in exchange for a commitment to guard the empire from further Viking attacks and Rollo's willingness to be baptized into the Christian faith. While remaining true to his commitment to keep other Vikings out of the area, Rollo and his descendants continued to expand their landholding in Normandy. Likewise, after years of raiding, the Vikings landed in England with a large army in 865 AD. After years of fighting, with both sides winning various battles, many Vikings did settle in England in an area that came to be known as Danelaw. This group of Vikings retained significant influence in England until 1066 AD, when the Norman king of Viking decent, William the Conqueror, expanded his territory into England as well.

In terms of their effect on Christian education, however, the Vikings frequently raided churches and monasteries, because these buildings contained money from tithes as

> The Viking raids had a decidedly negative effect on the availability of Christian education in that era

well as silver cups and ornaments used in worship. Scholars were also often taken as slaves in these raids. As a result, these raids had a decidedly negative effect on the availability of Christian education in that era. On the other hand, bringing so many Christian slaves and wives to their home country undoubtedly made the conversion of the Vikings to Christianity much easier, and many Viking kings eventually converted to Christianity.

England's King Alfred the Great was one bright spot in Christian education during the Viking era. The Vikings had decimated England's monasteries and churches, and Christian education had almost disappeared. After winning a number of decisive battles against the Vikings, he turned his attention to reviving education. King Alfred began by establishing a court school and recruiting renowned scholars from the mainland. He introduced English alongside Latin as a legitimate language of Christian education and encouraged the translation of important books into English.

The Holy Roman Empire and the Byzantine Empire both faced Magyar (Hungarian) invasions during this same time period. Like the Vikings, the Magyars attacked both Slavs and Germans to capture slaves to be sold to the Byzantine and Muslim empires. Magyars also joined the Moravian armies in some battles and then later defeated the Moravians. In the 900s, the Magyars invaded Italy, France, Spain, Germany, and the Byzantine Empire, taking loot and extorting "taxes." Like the Vikings, the Magyars settled down in conquered territory and eventually adopted European culture and the Christian faith around the end of this time period. Because monasteries and churches were easy and lucrative targets, the Magyar invasions also had a detrimental effect on Christian education, which was centered in these locations during this era.

The Islamic Arabs and Moors invaded Spain in 711 AD and quickly conquered most of the Iberian Peninsula. Over the next three hundred years, the majority of the population converted to Islam. A similar situation began in Sicily in 827 AD. These areas had been part of the Christian western division of the Roman Empire until its collapse, and the tribes that settled there after the collapse of the empire also converted to Christianity. Many Jews had also settled in Spain before it was conquered by the Muslims. While the Christians and Jews were not required to convert to Islam, they were treated as second class citizens under many of the Muslim rulers.

The Vikings gradually accepted Christianity in their homeland, beginning around 950 AD. However, many of the Viking settlers in the Christian parts of Europe had become Christians somewhat earlier. Viking conversions to Christianity appear to have come gradually both through evangelism among the common people as well as through political treaties with Christian rulers. It appears that many Vikings simply added Christianity to their pagan beliefs rather than giving up their pagan beliefs, so the true conversions to Christianity and the development of Christian education took many centuries.

One important historical marker in the Christianization of Viking lands was Danish King Cnut's visit to Rome in 1027 AD to attend the coronation of Conrad II as Holy Roman Emperor by Pope John XIX. This visit indicated that King Cnut was now accepted as a legitimate Christian king. From this time on, Cnut became a strong supporter of the Christian church in his lands.

While there had been valiant attempts to retain Christian education in Europe during the Viking era, this paradigm represents a significant decline in Christian education.

## Scholastic Paradigm

I believe that 1066 AD is the best marker for the end of the Viking age and the beginning of the next paradigm. That year the Anglo-Saxon king, Harold Godwinson, fought off the last significant Viking invasion of England, only to be defeated a few weeks later at the Battle of Hastings by William the Conqueror from Normandy, who was also of Viking decent. A potentially significant attack led by King Cnut IV of Denmark in 1083 ended with a whimper. As the Viking tribes transformed into Christian Scandinavian nations, the Viking era came to an end.

However, other authors, such as Phyllis Tickle, suggest that the Great Schism of 1054 is the best marker for the transition of paradigms. After years of increasing theological and political tension between the leaders of the Latin Christian church based in Rome and the leaders of the Greek Christian church based in Constantinople, these two entities parted company on less than friendly terms. After this division, the Roman popes exerted significantly more authority over both the Christian church and the political sphere in Europe. Either date is appropriate, since paradigm shifts do not usually happen overnight.

Pope Urban II exercised this increased authority to call western Europe's political and military leaders to liberate the Holy Land from Muslim control, and his doing so launched the First Crusade in 1095 AD. The immediate trigger for this crusade was a petition from the Byzantine emperor for military aid to push back the Muslim Turks who had been gradually gaining ground in Asia Minor at the expense of the Byzantines. Pope Urban II urged the Latin Christians to participate in an armed pilgrimage to Jerusalem in response to the Byzantine request. The crusaders did succeed in setting up several crusader states in the Holy Land and retained a Christian political presence there for a few hundred years.

The knights from Latin Europe played a significant role in the crusades and appear to have elevated their status as a result. Charlemagne had already made significant use of mounted warriors and granted them land in exchange for faithful service. Over time, these mounted warriors developed into a class of respected knights. By the time of the crusades, these knights had proved themselves in battle against the Vikings and Magyars. The church often spoke up against the knights' abuses against women and civilians, but happily recruited them for the crusades. Many of the crusader knights came from Viking backgrounds. The crusaders were able to channel their restless, violent energy into acceptable and even admirable exploits on behalf of the church. The Latin church also created several religious orders of knights to protect pilgrims traveling to holy sites in Jerusalem and elsewhere and required the knights in these orders to accept various Christian disciplines.

Over time, a whole tradition developed around apprenticing the sons of knights and lords for knighthood. These boys typically lived with their mothers or foster mothers in castles until age six and then became pages at age seven. At the page stage, boys would receive a Christian spiritual and academic education from a priest or chaplain, as well as learn hunting skills. Pages would also accompany knights into battle, carrying baggage, cleaning armour, and looking after horses. Older pages were taught combat using wooden swords and spears. At age fifteen, the pages would go through a religious ceremony to become squires. At this stage, the youths would learn to dance, wrestle, fence, long jump, ride, swim, climb, and participate in tournaments, all while wearing their own real armour. Squires were also required to learn the code of chivalry, which they had to take in an oath at their knighting ceremony at age twenty-one. By incorporating religious instruction into this apprenticeship for knighthood, the church was able to redirect the violent energy of boys into protecting the churches as well as the weak and defenceless people in their society. The crusades played a significant role in this transformation.

The crusades also brought Europeans into contact with the more advanced Byzantine and Muslim cultures. In the fourth crusade, the Europeans stormed Constantinople and weakened it to the point where it could no longer defend itself well against the Muslim Turks. While this was a loss for Christianity as a whole, it was a gain for the Latin church, as we will see in the next paradigm.

This time period produced a number of influential scholastic thinkers. Archbishop Lanfranc of Canterbury (1005–1089 AD) was already well-known for his lectures on the trivium of grammar, logic, and rhetoric in France before being made Archbishop of Canterbury. Archbishop Anselm of Canterbury (1033–1109 AD) taught that while faith must precede reason, reason can expand upon faith. He is considered by some writers to be the greatest intellect between St. Augustine and St. Thomas Aquinas, and the father of scholasticism. Peter Abelard (1079–1142 AD) contributed to scholarship in metaphysics, logic, philosophy of language, philosophy of mind, ethics, and theology. Alexander of Hales (1185–1245 AD) was one of the first teachers to refer to Aristotle's works, which had recently been translated into Latin. In this regard, Alexander of Hales is a transitional figure, foreshadowing the Renaissance.

Scholasticism, and the teaching of St. Thomas Aquinas in particular, has had a continuing influence on Christian education. In Scholasticism, students are required to use the Bible, the teachings of church leaders, reason, and experience to debate apparent contradictions in order to reconcile these contradictions. One significant focus of scholasticism was to try to reconcile Christian belief with classical Greek thought. Within scholasticism, the various academic subjects were all subtopics of Christian theology. Some elements of scholasticism, such as the infusion of faith into all subjects as well as Socratic dialogue, are still present in Christian education today. The Scholastic teaching on God's transcendental qualities of truth, goodness, and beauty is still present in the Catholic catechism.

> Scholasticism, and the teaching of St. Thomas Aquinas in particular, has had a continuing influence on Christian education.

Later Scholastic thinkers, such as William of Ockham, disconnected investigations such as science from theology, and most Christian educators have resisted this separation of academic investigation from theology. However, this disconnection remains in many Christians' thinking to this day.

Since Scholasticism was developed in monastic and church schools, the focus of education was on training church leaders. Over time, however, both political and civic leaders sent their children to these schools for training. Scholastic education formed part of the training of knights described above.

> The Scholastic paradigm should be thought of as a time of resurgence of Christian education both in theological depth as well as in the spread of Christian education through the training of political and civic leaders.

In summary, the Scholastic paradigm should be thought of as a time of resurgence of Christian education both in theological depth as well as in the spread of Christian education through the training of political and civic leaders, including knights.

Vic Wiens

## Renaissance Paradigm

While the Renaissance is generally viewed as starting in Italy around 1350 AD, the roots of the Renaissance date to 1204 AD and the Fourth Crusade. What is frequently called the High Middle Ages is really the first stage of the Renaissance when viewing history through the lens of paradigm change, because this entire time period was heavily influenced by Greek culture.

After the fall of Rome in 476, the Eastern Roman Empire, with Byzantium as its capital, retained most of its territory and even retook parts of the lost Western Roman Empire. This Byzantine Empire survived for about one thousand years after the fall of Rome. Over time, however, this Christian Greek Byzantine Empire had already experienced a number of serious setbacks at the hands of the expanding Muslim Turks. As a result, this empire requested the help of the Christian kingdoms of Europe to expel the Turks. The Christian European kingdoms accepted this mission, with the goal of capturing the Holy Land from the Muslims to set up a Christian state there. This triggered a series of somewhat successful military crusades from Europe. However, the European kingdoms were not really intent on helping the Byzantine Empire, since they were in economic competition with this wealthy empire. In fact, it was the actions of the Christian European kingdoms, and in particular the sack of Byzantium in 1204 AD by the crusaders, that significantly weakened the Byzantine Empire.

While this was a significant blow to Christian education in the Byzantine Empire, it was a gain for Christian education in Europe. From this point on, the Europeans bought and stole many Greek Christian and pagan

> While the weakening of the Byzantine Empire was a significant blow to Christian education in that empire, it was a gain for Christian education in Europe.

manuscripts and artifacts from the Byzantines. The Europeans were also able to attract many Greek scholars from the shrinking Byzantine

Empire. This kindled a powerful interest in both literary and artistic classical studies in Europe, and especially in Italy.

The Renaissance had a significant impact on Christian education in Europe. While Scholastic education focused on reason, Renaissance education focused on humanism. While Scholastic education was God focused, humanistic education was people focused, following the Greek and Roman models.

In the Renaissance, thinkers were eager to read original sources, so many classical Greek manuscripts that had been read only in Latin up until that time were studied in their original Greek language. Since the Greeks viewed humankind as the measure of all things, this study of classical Greek manuscripts very naturally led to a more human orientation in education as well.

While the Scholastics emphasized the truth aspect of the triad of truth, goodness, and beauty, the humanists emphasised the beauty aspect. Art, literature, and architecture were heavily influenced by emulation of classical Greek forms. Art became more realistic, following the Greek tradition. Many paintings and sculptures from this period followed the Greek depiction of nudes. Even religious art in this period often included both male and female nudes, and live art models became an integral part of producing art. The use of live art models in university art classes has continued to the current time, even in a number of Christian universities.

Renaissance humanistic education included allowing students to form their own opinions, and teachers became more focused on creating comfortable and caring learning environments. The concept of differentiating instruction based

> Humanities: Those branches of knowledge that concern themselves with human beings and their culture.
>
> *Britannica*

on different learning styles was already present in Renaissance education. Students were encouraged to become well-rounded human beings, and we still use the term "Renaissance man" to describe people who are particularly well-rounded in their interests and accomplishments. We also still talk about the "humanities" in contemporary education.

While classical rhetoric had not been completely lost since the classical Greek and Roman period, the Renaissance renewed this as an emphasis. Renaissance students were not only encouraged to develop their own opinions about various topics, but also to be able to persuade others of the correctness of their opinions.

Since humanistic education encouraged students to develop their own opinions, it is not surprising that there were numerous smaller Church reform movements in the Renaissance period prior to the Reformation. All of these early reformers highly valued Christian education in some form.

> Since humanistic education encouraged students to develop their own opinions, it is not surprising that there were numerous smaller Church reform movements in the Renaissance.

John Wycliffe (1329–1384) is sometimes referred to as the "Morning Star" of the Reformation. As the leading theologian of Europe's leading university, Oxford University in England, Wycliffe was concerned that the ordinary people of England could not read the Bible in their own language. As a result, he translated the Bible into common English, and this Bible was distributed around the time of his death. However, because his translation predated the printing press, only a few people were able to access this hand-copied English Bible. His followers became known as the Lollards after his death, and they encouraged people to learn to read English so they could read the Bible in their own language. Many of the Lollards were martyred for their evangelical faith.

John Huss (1373–1415) was the president of the Catholic University of Prague in what is now the Czech Republic. Because Huss encouraged people to read the writings of John Wycliffe, he was removed from his office and excommunicated from the Catholic Church. He went into exile and continued to write, developing a significant following. Although Huss was burned at the stake for his "heretical" views, his followers, known as Hussites and later the Moravians, continued to multiply.

These and other pre-Reformation leaders became champions of vernacular Bible translations and of basic literacy for all, so that the common people could read the Bible in their own language. They also emphasized instruction in the catechism. By the time of the Reformation, there were hundreds of Christian schools scattered throughout Europe. Many of these schools were small and often met in people's homes. The Hussites (Moravians) had already translated and printed the Bible in the vernacular, developed a system of elementary and secondary schools, and even established a university prior to the Reformation. In spite of intense persecution, they were operating about three hundred churches and three hundred schools by the time of the Lutheran Reformation.

Martin Luther attended another significant pre-Reformation Christian school system, operated by the Brethren of the Common Life. The Brethren of the Common Life schools were founded by Gerard Groote and remained Catholic even though they were relatively evangelical in nature. By the time of the Reformation, they were operating hundreds of schools throughout western Europe.

The leaders of the Reformation borrowed heavily from all of these Renaissance period pre-Reformation forms of Christian education.

## Reformation Paradigm

The date usually given for the start of the Reformation paradigm is October 31, 1517. This was the day that Martin Luther nailed his 95 Theses to the Whittenburg church door in an attempt to argue for the correction of what he saw as being significant errors in the teachings of the Catholic Church in his day. Luther, a theology professor at the Whittenburg University, had followed the Renaissance tradition of reading original Greek sources and had formed his own opinions. He had also learned the value of debate from the Scholastic tradition.

We have already viewed the historical context of the Reformation in our discussion of the nature of paradigm shifts, so in this section I would like to focus on the discipleship of children and youth of believers in the

Reformation era. Luther, Calvin, and Knox, three of the key leaders in the Reformation, determined to rebuild what they saw as the vibrant early church era. As they studied the early church writings in the original Greek manuscripts, they determined that Christian education in that early church era had consisted of a three-pronged approach consisting of the home, church, and

> The Reformers believed that parents needed to take ultimate responsibility for the Christian education of their children, but they also believed that the church needed to provide instruction in the catechism and that the school needed to provide a broader, Christ-centered education.

school. While their approaches differed to some degree, all three Reformers implemented this three-pronged approach.

The Reformers believed that parents needed to take ultimate responsibility for the Christian education of their children, but they also believed that the church needed to provide instruction in the catechism and that the school needed to provide a broader, Christ-centered education. They believed that the sad condition of the church in their time was largely a result of negligence in all three educational prongs.

Calvin, for example, used a three-prong approach to Christian education for the city-state of Geneva. First, he directed pastors, and later their assistants, to teach the catechism to children and required the children to be able to answer the catechism questions before being admitted as full members of the church. Second, he directed parents to make their faith personally applicable to their children. Thirdly, he organized schools to teach children to read and write as well as learn about the world more broadly; for older students, he organized a secondary school and a university.

Luther, Calvin, and Knox were extraordinarily strong proponents of church catechisms and Christian schooling. Luther tried to institute mandatory basic Christian education for everyone. This education focused on learning to read the Bible and stories that supported the teachings of the Bible and learning the catechism. He also advocated secondary education for more capable students. This education was broader and included languages, literature, history, mathematics, natural sciences, music, and gymnastics. In broadening the curriculum, he broke away from the early church tradition of teaching only the Scriptures, and in many respects adopted the Byzantine model of Christian classical education for secondary students. He also extended his program of education to include Christian universities, again following the Byzantine tradition. However, at the end of his life, Luther bemoaned the limited impact his educational reforms had on the spiritual lives of people in the Lutheran lands.

John Calvin (and his counterpart in Scotland, John Knox) saw the church and the school as two branches of the same ministry. Calvin strongly believed that there should be no division between secular and sacred, so he was very inclusive in his school curriculum. On Sundays, however, the focus was on learning the catechism in the church. Many authors treat the Sunday School movement as a new innovation of the 1700s, but in reality, all of the reformers had already implemented some version of Sunday School. Calvin, for example, implemented his Sunday catechism program as a direct replication of what he understood had happened in the early church.

John Knox applied the principles he learned from John Calvin on a national level in the Scottish Lowlands. He insisted that there should be a church and a Christian school in every community, and every church had to appoint a schoolmaster, even if that position had to be filled by the pastor. Through Knox's efforts, the peasants in the Scottish Lowlands became the most educated in the world. Like Luther, Calvin and Knox broke away from the early church tradition of teaching only the Scriptures. Like Luther, they also extended their educational programs to include secondary programs and Christian universities.

The Calvinist reformation also took hold in Holland. At the Dutch Synod of Dort (1618–1619), Reformed Church leaders articulated the Dort Education Policy, excerpts of which are quoted here:

**The 1618 Dort Education Policy (Abbreviated)** *In order that the Christian youth may be diligently instructed in the principles of religion and be trained in piety, three modes of catechizing should be employed.*

I. *In the houses, by parents.*

II. *In the schools, by schoolmasters.*

III. *In the churches, by ministers, elders and catechists especially appointed for the purpose.*

> *The office of parents is to diligently instruct their children and their whole household in the principles of the Christian religion, in a manner adapted to their respective capacities ....*

> *Schools, in which the young shall be properly instructed in the principles of Christian doctrine, shall be instituted not only in cities, but also in towns and country places where heretofore none have existed. ... That well-qualified persons may be employed and enabled to devote themselves to the service; and especially that the children of the poor may be gratuitously instructed, and not be excluded from the benefit of the schools ....*

> *In order that due knowledge may be obtained of the diligence of the schoolmasters, and the improvement of the youth, it shall be the duty of the ministers, with an elder ... to visit all the schools ....*

From Frederick Eby and Charles Flinn Arrowood, *The Development of Modern Education* (New York: Prentice Hall, 1934), pp. 168–169.

The Church of England (Anglican Church) was founded by a king rather than a theological reformer. However, there were a number of reformers both inside and outside the Anglican Church in England. These dissenters were often the ones to migrate to the New England colonies. It was these dissenters, like the Puritans, who placed the highest value on education.

The Protestant Reformation also triggered what is often referred to by Protestants as the Counter-Reformation within the Roman Catholic Church. Catholics prefer to simply call it the Roman Catholic Reformation. This movement also included the proliferation of Catholic schools, which we still see around the world today. As of 2016, there were 43,800 Catholic secondary schools and 95,200 Catholic elementary around the world.

These Protestant and Catholic reformers all favored state churches. Even the English dissenters created the equivalent of state churches in their New England colonies. The reformers also all saw education as essential to maintaining their faith in their countries and their colonies. Even the Church of England, which was slow to reform, got on the education bandwagon in 1701 with the founding of The Society for the Propagation of the Gospel in Foreign Parts. This organization was created largely for the purpose of bringing the dissenters back into the Anglican fold and bringing the Anglican gospel to Indians and slaves. In spite of great efforts, these goals were not accomplished, although many existing Anglicans received their education through the efforts of this organization.

The Anabaptists formed the radical wing of the Reformation, and they did not believe in a state church or in infant baptism. This group included both the Mennonites and the Baptists, among others. Because they were persecuted by all of the state churches, they were forced to keep a low profile and operated primarily out of homes. As a result, there was not such a clear distinction between the three prongs of Christian education.

However, when the Mennonites did achieve religious freedom, as they did when a group migrated to Pennsylvania, they were equally focused on establishing Christian schools. As Mennonite historian C. Henry Smith explains:

> The Mennonites are often accused by those who know
> them least of being opposed to learning. This is not

the case. In the early colonial days in Pennsylvania, the Mennonites were among the first to make provision for the education of their boys and girls … and many of the early meeting houses … also served as schoolhouses.

C. Henry Smith, "Christopher Dock: The Pious Schoolmaster of Skippack," *Christian Monitor* I (January 1909), p. 18, quoted by Kienel, p. 120.

Mennonites also migrated to other countries and typically set up colonies, or Mennonite-only communities, as they had done in America. Although they did not believe in state churches, their colonies operated in a state-like manner, where all community members attended the same church, and children attended the same school staffed by Mennonite teachers.

During this era, Christianity spread around the world. In the same way that the printing press technology had allowed for the spread of Reformation ideas and for the printing of the Bible, technological advances in sailing ships allowed Europeans to explore the world. Not long before the Reformation, the Portuguese had established trading posts around Africa and in India, and Columbus had discovered America. Wherever the Europeans went, they established colonies and their state or state-like churches.

British North America was an anomaly because of the range of church denominations that were permitted to exist alongside each other. While the settlers of these various denominations initially largely kept to themselves and established the equivalent of state churches in their areas, this mix of denominations would lead to some significant changes to Christian education in the future.

## Modern Paradigm

We have already noted that secular public education is a product of the next major paradigm change, triggered by the Enlightenment, the Industrial Revolution, and extensive globalization roughly 250 years ago. This era is generally known as the Modern era. While the reformers sought to erase the distinction between the sacred and secular, many of the Enlightenment thinkers sought to secularize knowledge. The eventual secularization of public elementary, secondary, and university education in our culture is a direct consequence of the Enlightenment. The Great Awakenings, which happened around the same time, were a significant contrast to the Enlightenment, as they brought a renewal of Christian fervor in America that impacted the world spiritually throughout the Modern era. The Industrial Revolution, which occurred at the same time, changed the nature of work, and therefore also of education. This has impacted Christian education as much as the philosophical and religious movements have.

While Europe still has remnants of state church education, America, in particular, does not. As a result, our discussion here will focus on the American scene first, since it is the fullest expression of education in general, and Christian education in particular, in the Modern era.

The thirteen British colonies that formed the core of the United States of America represented a range of religious tradition, even more so after the Great Awakenings. The USA conducted the first national experiment of applying Enlightenment thinking to government, and the Industrial Revolution came to America at about the same time that the thirteen British colonies became an independent nation. As a result, we can see the fullest expression of these cultural influences in this country and the subsequent fullest expressions of Christian education.

The Great Awakenings made a significant positive impact on Christianity. The Great Awakenings

This diversity of denominations opened the Christian community up to more pluralistic forms of education, which subsequently led to the secularization of publicly funded education.

produced much higher levels of personal faith commitment and also produced many faith-based schools at every level. However, they also further fragmented the American faith community, making denominational Christian schools much more difficult since there were often not enough students from each denomination to justify separate denominational schools. This diversity of denominations opened the Christian community up to more pluralistic forms of education, which subsequently led to the secularization of publicly funded education.

Because the Great Awakening was linked to the Pietist movement in western Europe, it is not surprising that Christian education in America was deeply influenced by Pietist forms of education. By the time the Pietist movement impacted education in America, it had combined the influences of several important Christian leaders. Lutheran pastor and theologian Philipp Spener is generally viewed as the father of Pietism through his preaching and writing in the late 1600s. The focus of his work was to emphasize individual personal transformation through spiritual rebirth and renewal. When Spener died in 1705, August Francke became the most influential Pietist leader. Francke is best known for his Francke Foundations, constructed just outside the city of Halle, which included a school for the poor, an orphanage, a medical dispensary, and a publishing house.

These schools inspired Frederick the Great of Prussia (the largest German state) to institute the first government funded public school system based on the Francke and Comenius model in 1763, at the very beginning of the Industrial Revolution. He could see how these practically oriented schools would enhance Prussia's economy. These publicly funded schools continued to teach Christian education as part of their required curriculum. In fact, they still do to some extent in Germany, to the dismay of non-Christians and Christians of differing faith backgrounds.

Spener was also a godfather to Count von Zinzendorf, who subsequently became the leader of the Moravian Brethren at his community of Herrnhut on his hereditary estate in Saxony. This is an amazing story of its own. When Zinzendorf met two refugees from Moravia who were fleeing persecution for their Protestant faith, he invited them to bring their persecuted friends to come live on his estate in Germany. He also invited persecuted Pietists to join this community. Through his leadership of this community and its missional activities, Zinzendorf become one of the most influential Pietist leaders. Zinzendorf also incorporated many ideas of the earlier Moravian writer John Amos Comenius, who had written extensively about Christian education. Whereas Luther and Calvin had emphasized classical education, Comenius and Francke introduced many more practical courses into the Christian school curriculum. Both the emphasis on a personalized faith and these practical courses found their way into Christian schools in America through the Great Awakenings, which were heavily influenced by German Pietism.

As we have seen, Christian education in the thirteen British colonies in America prior to this era was church based, and it included the home, church, and Christian school, regardless of religious tradition. However, as the Christian community fragmented into multiple denominations, that model was no longer effective. The first solution to this fragmentation was the "common school" movement, which was primarily focused on elementary education. Common schools were typically operated by religious societies and were open to children of all denominations. These schools were typically funded by a combination of tuition, private philanthropy, and local taxes. Because not all families could afford tuition, societies were formed to raise enough funds through various levels of government as well as private philanthropy to operate free common schools where they were most needed.

> The first solution to this fragmentation was the "common school" movement, which was primarily focused on elementary education.

After the founding of the common schools for elementary aged children, many church denominations focused on secondary and postsecondary education. These denominational private "academies" and evangelical colleges flourished for many years in America. Interestingly,

Benjamin Franklin, who was not a believer, set up an academy in Philadelphia that reflected the more practical orientation of Comenius and Francke. Most of the Christian academies followed this same practical pattern. Over time, many of these academies opened up to students from other

> After the founding of the common schools for elementary aged children, many church denominations focused on secondary and postsecondary education.

denominations as well, and in many cases eventually became interdenominational schools.

As Roman Catholic immigration increased in the 1800s and as the more historically Spanish Catholic states such as Florida, Louisiana, New Mexico, and California joined the USA, Catholic education became a significant component of Christian education in America. According to Catholic Church historian John Gilmary Shea, over twelve million Catholics had immigrated to America by the end of the nineteenth century. The significant immigration of Catholics together with the increasing secularization of public education resulted in a significant effort on the part of the Catholic churches in America to develop and promote Catholic schools by the early 1900s.

For comparison's sake, at this same time, comparable forms of Christian education were developed in Great Britain. The British "public schools" were the equivalent of the American common schools and nondenominational academies, except they did not receive any tax revenue, and therefore were more expensive and exclusive. These were public in the sense that they were operated by societies rather than churches and that they were open to children from all denominations. The Sunday School movement started in Great Britain to provide a basic Christian education for children of families who could not afford to pay the public school tuitions.

In 1837, the term "public school" took on a different meaning in America when the first fully tax-supported system of free schools was established in Massachusetts. Eight of eleven members of the initial school board of this first American public school system were Unitarians, who were viewed as heretical by most other Christian denominations, because they no longer believed in the Trinity or the deity of Jesus Christ. While the Bible was to be read daily in these public schools, it was to be read without comment so as not to promote the teachings of any particular

> Many states permitted what became known as "common doctrine" schools which referred to the commonly held doctrines of mainstream evangelical churches.

church. Although these public schools were officially based on a general Judeo-Christian worldview, in fact, they were rapidly secularized because of the strong liberal leanings of the Unitarian leaders.

Over time, many states adopted legislation to forbid sectarian instruction in public schools. However, many states permitted what became known as "common doctrine," which referred to the commonly held doctrines of mainstream evangelical churches. Church groups often cooperated in developing these common doctrinal statements, which could be used in schools in a similar way in which they had done earlier in the independent common schools. The Sunday School movement was re-envisioned to provide teaching on the more unique doctrines of their church denominations on Sundays. It was on this basis that public schools were supported by many church leaders. While this compromise model was never as effective as the Christian school model that preceded it, the common doctrine model combined with the newly re-envisioned Sunday School programs served Christians adequately for about one hundred years.

However, not all church denominations accepted the common doctrine compromise. While Christian academies (high schools) were already in existence before the public school movement, they came to be viewed as providing an important truly Christian option after the increase of public schools. By 1850, more than seven thousand Christian academies had been established around the country, although many of these did not survive the disruption of the Civil War. Roman Catholics,

Lutherans, and Dutch Calvinists were not satisfied with the common doctrine compromise and continued to operate their own schools.

The American Bible school movement began shortly after the end of the American Civil War as a reaction to the increasing secularization of higher education. Historians generally give credit to A. B. Simpson, founder of the Christian and Missionary Alliance movement, for starting the first Bible school, Nyack College, in 1882. Moody Bible Institute was opened by evangelist D. L. Moody in 1887. These two schools served as both the models and training grounds for hundreds of other Bible institutes and colleges. In many churches, young people who had received minimal Christian education due to the secularization of public education made up for lost ground by spending one or more years studying the Bible in one of these Bible institutes. The first Bible institutes in Canada were opened in the late 1880s and early 1890s and were modeled after Nyack and Moody.

John Dewey initiated the Progressive Education movement, which gained momentum in American public schools in the first half of the twentieth century. Dewey was a vocal humanist, and he pushed very hard for the full secularization of American public education. Then in 1947, the Supreme Court interpreted Thomas Jefferson's comments on the separation of church and state to mean that religion had no place in public education. In many respects, that date officially ended the era of the common doctrine, which had been significantly watered down by then. Subsequent court rulings in the 1960s removed public prayer from public schools as well. These rulings became the symbolic end of the common doctrine era. Unfortunately, the support by many church leaders for the public school system has not changed, even though the common doctrine era has completely ended.

The symbolic end of the common doctrine era did provide the impetus for a new Christian school movement. We will look at this new movement and several new models of Christian education in a later chapter, but here we will look at the Christian education landscape at the end of the Modern era.

According to the Guide2Research (https://research.com/research/american-school-statistics), by 2020 around 90 percent of American elementary and secondary students attended public schools.

> This means that the historic Christian formula of home, church, and school has broken down.

By law, American public schools are required to be secular. On the other hand, based on "America's Changing Religious Landscape," Pew Research Center: Religion & Public Life. May 12, 2015, around 75 percent of Americans claimed to be Christians in 2015. This has significant implications for Christian education because it means that the historic Christian formula of home, church, and school has broken down.

On the positive side, Christian schools continue to make a difference for the minority of Christian families who make them a priority. According to the *2018 US Cardus Education Survey: Spiritual Strength, Faithful Formation*, Protestant Christian school and religious homeschool graduates, compared to public and non-religious private school graduates:

- more consistently believe that Jesus Christ is the only way to salvation
- are more committed to their churches, practice spiritual disciplines more frequently, and are following church teachings at much higher rates
- hold more strongly to the belief that morality is unchanging and absolute
- make family a top priority, including having more children and divorcing less frequently
- retain their belief in the infallibility of the Bible
- give more money to their churches and to other charitable causes

In summary, this Cardus study found that "on every measure of traditional religious beliefs, Protestant Christian school graduates show significantly more adherence to the church teachings that their peers, findings that hold up after rigorous controls ...." Graduates of the religious homeschool category came second on most measures.

However, the majority of Protestant families do not send their children to private Protestant schools or provide Christian home-based education. What is of even greater concern is that the majority of Protestant pastors do not teach parents the importance of sending children to private Protestant Christian schools or providing Christian homeschooling, nor do most pastor training programs teach them to do so.

The same Cardus research found that Catholic schools were somewhat effective by those same measures, but not as effective as Protestant Christian schools and religious home school contexts. It should be noted, however, that Catholic home school students were included in the religious home school category. Catholic homeschooling does appear to be highly effective in faith transmission, and likely the most effective current option for Catholic families. However, I have not found research that is specific to Catholic homeschooling.

We know, then, that the school part of the Christian education triad had broken down for most Christian families. But have the home and church picked up the slack? While around 75 percent of Americans claim to be Christians, according to research by the Barna organization (https://www.barna.com/research), only 31 percent attend church at least once per month. This means that the church part of the triad may be just as broken as the school part. According to the Cardus Education Survey (https://www.cardus.ca/research/education/cardus-education-survey), it is the graduates of Protestant Christian schools who are more likely to be attending church regularly. This means that the impact of church-based Christian education on children not attending Christian schools is likely even lower, because they are also less likely to be attending church. If my own church experience over the last forty years in five healthy churches is at all representative, among those families who considered our church their church home, the average attendance is only about twice a month. This means children are typically receiving about two to three hours of faith-based instruction in church compared to about one hundred hours of secular school instruction each month.

However, not all churches have limited their faith-based instruction to their weekend church services. I will highlight a few of the most effective additional programs that arose in this previous era. I will comment on their effectiveness from my own observations.

- Weekday catechism classes became an important form of faith transfer in many churches. Besides providing for more hours of faith instruction in a given week, weekday catechism classes allow trained pastors to lead the classes at a time when they are not feeling the pressure of leading church services. Some churches provide focused weekday classes specifically for children who are attending public schools. This is consistent with the early church model where both children who did not attend the Christian schools and new adult believers received two to three years of such weekly instruction in the catechism before being able to fully participate in church life. Unfortunately, these weekday catechism classes are rare.

- Weekday club programs such as Boys Brigade, Pioneer Girls, Awana, GEMS, and Cadets provide children with additional Christian instruction and activities. Unfortunately, many churches dropped these programs due to a shortage of volunteers and conflicting community sports programs. Where these have been discontinued, they have left a significant void.

- Vacation Bible School, summer backyard clubs, summer day camp programs, and off-site summer camp programs are often focused on both faith-based instruction for church families and as outreach activities for children from non-church families. In my experience, these programs are effective at challenging children to make personal faith commitments, but children need to find their way into weekly church, Sunday School, and weekday club programs to make the commitments lasting. These programs so often fail to facilitate this transition.

Overall, even when children who do attend public schools have the opportunity to participate in multiple church-based programs, they receive minimal faith-based instruction relative to the public school and media influences in their lives. These weekday Christian educations programs have also seen a significant drop in attendance as community sports and fine arts activities have become a higher priority, even for Christian families.

The Bible school movement has also faded, or at least has morphed. Many of the smaller Bible institutes either closed or merged with other schools. The establishment of the Association for Biblical Higher Education in 1947 gave these schools more formal external academic standards to strive toward, and this had both a positive and negative effect. On the positive side, this accreditation process raised the academic level of both the courses and the instructors. On the negative side, many Bible institutes either closed due to their inability to meet the accreditation standards or transitioned into Christian liberal arts colleges with less biblical leanings. Bible institutes and colleges no longer attract the significant numbers of young adults that they did in years gone by.

On the other hand, a new variety of more experiential Christian education programs are being developed to disciple recent high school graduates. We will leave the discussion on these new programs for our discussion of the new paradigm in Christian education in a future book.

So if the school part and the church part of the triad have broken down, what about the family part of this triad?

One relatively recent book, *Families and Faith: How Religion is Passed Down Across Generations,* by Bengtson, Putney, and Harris, indicates that some families remain relatively effective in passing on their faith, while other parents are doing poorly. This book, based on a longitudinal study over thirty-five years, indicates that the closeness children feel to their parents is one of the most significant factors determining whether children adopt the faith of their parents. Their study also found that "having a close bond with one's *father* matters even more than a close relationship with the mother," for Christian families. However, this close relationship with the father can also have the effect of following a father into non-involvement with a faith community.

On a positive note, grandparents play an increasingly important role in faith transmission as life expectancy increases. The Bengtson, Putney, and Harris study also found that new communication technologies have allowed grandparents to remain emotionally closer to their grandchildren when they live in distant communities. Based on this study, it appears that grandmothers play just as effective a role in faith transmission as grandfathers. However, these close relationships can also have the effect of following grandparents into non-involvement with a faith community.

This study also found that both interfaith marriages and divorces significantly undermined faith transmission. However, when interfaith marriages result in choosing and committing to some common faith, the transmission process strengthens. In this study, fathers in interfaith marriages were very often non-believers, which significantly hampered the mothers' ability to pass on their faith.

Other research corroborates these findings. For example, in his June 18, 2015, Fathers' Day blog entry titled, "Dad Matters!... The Spiritual Influence of Fathers" (https://formingfaith.blog/2015/06/18/dad-matters-the-spiritual-influence-of-fathers ), the anonymous Lutheran pastor refers to a Swiss study in 1994, which reported in a January 2000 article by Werner Haug and Phillipe Warner that fathers played a more significant role in subsequent church attendance than mothers and that the negligence of fathers in the spiritual development of their children was a very significant factor in the failure of families to pass their faith on to the next generation.

This same blog post refers to the research-based article by Boyatzis, Dollahite, and Marks, titled "The Family as a Context for Religious and Spiritual Development in Children and Youth," published in *The Handbook of Spiritual Development in Childhood and Adolescence*. This research found that mothers had almost two and a half times more faith related conversations with their children than fathers. They also reported that mothers attended worship services more often, and adults could remember their mothers praying more often than their fathers.

My own impression from personal observation combined with the research is that Christian fathers are not necessarily more reluctant to pass on their faith to their children than in previous eras, but rather that our current culture requires a significantly higher level of commitment to push past obstacles in order to do so. While fathers spent more time with their children, and especially their sons, working together on family farms and in family businesses in previous eras, most fathers now work away from home. Fathers now have to be much more deliberate in carving out time for spiritual conversations with their children.

Regardless of where the blame lies, families have not been effective in passing their faith on to the next generation. The parent part of the home, school, and church triad is needing to be strengthened.

This does not mean that there are no good examples of the triad of home, school, and church working together effectively at the end of the Modern era. The research points to the triad of involved fathers, involved churches, and private Christian schools as having been the most effective combination in the last era. Various forms of Christian, home-based schooling also show significant promise. Unfortunately, these good examples are not the norm.

## Christian Education in The New Paradigm

The mandate to pass on our Christian faith to the next generation does not change with paradigm shifts in culture. In this overview of how God's people have passed on their faith in previous cultural paradigm shifts, we see that there are both continuities and discontinuities in practice.

The role of parents—and especially that of fathers—appears to be the most significant continuity as we look toward the new paradigm we are entering. For all the changes in church and school programs through the various paradigms, we see that fathers continue to play a pivotal role in Christian education. As a grandfather, I have been impressed with the historic role of the patriarch in passing on the faith. It is in my role as family patriarch that I need to resonate with Joshua when he stated emphatically, "But as for me and my household, we will serve the Lord" (Josh. 24:15b). How do we fill in the gap created by so many absent fathers and grandfathers, as well as fathers and grandfathers who do not set a healthy example of living the Christian life?

The triad of home, church, and Christian school is the second significant theme that runs through over two thousand years of passing on the faith to future generations. Have churches lost their commitment to supporting this triad? What forms will this triad take with the significant changes that accompany paradigm shifts in culture? Does the relative effectiveness of religious homeschooling potentially replace the triad with a duo?

I have intentionally focused this book exclusively on the history of paradigm changes in Christian education, since this history helps us gain perspective or options for the future. I am already working on series of books to address these and many other questions. I have already noted that we are now well into the transition period from the Modern paradigm to a yet-to-be named new cultural paradigm. This new cultural paradigm, the new forms of parenting, and the Christian education triad will likely become clearer even as I continue writing.

# Bibliography

America's Changing Religious Landscape. *Religion and Public Life.* Washington, DC: Pew Research Center, May 12, 2015.

Arnall, Judy. *Unschooling to University: Relationships Matter Most in a World Crammed with Content.* Calgary, Alberta: Professional Parenting, 2018.

Asbridge, Thomas. *The Crusades: The Authoritative History of the War for the Holy Land.* London: Simon and Schuster, 2020.

Bakke, O.M., translated by Brian McNeil. *When Children Became People: The Birth of Childhood in Early Christianity.* Minneapolis: Fortress Press, 2005.

Barna, George. *The Second Coming of the Church: A Blueprint for Survival.* Nashville, Tennessee: Word Publishing, 1998.

Bartlett, W.B. *Vikings: A History of the Northmen.* The Hill, Stroud Gloucestershire: Amberley Publishing, 2019.

Bengtson, Vern L., Norella M. Putney, and Susan Harris. *Families and Faith: How Religion is Passed Down Across Generations.* Oxford, England: Oxford University Press, 2017.

Boyatzis, Chris, David C. Dollahite, and Loren D. Marks. The Family as a Context for Religious and Spiritual Development in Children and Youth. In Roehlkepartain, Eugene, Pamela Ebstyne, Linda Wagner, and Peter Benson,

(Ed.). *The Handbook of Spiritual Development in Childhood and Adolescence*. Thousand Oaks, CA: Sage Publications, 2005.

Brinton, Crane, John B. Christopher, and Robert Lee Wolff. *Civilization in the West, 3rd Edition*. Englewood Cliffs, New Jersey: Prentice Hall, 1973.

*Cardus US 2018 Education Survey: Spiritual Strength, Faithful Formation*. Hamilton, Ontario: Cardus Research, 2018.

Christiansen, Clayton M. and Curtis W. Johnson. *Disrupting Class: How Disruptive Innovation Will Change the Way the World Learns*. New York: McGraw-Hill, 2008.

Dad Matters: The Spiritual Influence of Fathers, *Forming Faith Blog*. June 18, 2015.

Dobbs, Richard, James Manyika, and Jonathan Woetzel. *No Ordinary Disruption: The Four Global Forces Breaking all the Trends*. New York: Public Affairs, 2015.

Drucker, Peter F. *The Landmarks of Tomorrow*. New York: Harper Press, 1959.

Durant, Will. *The Renaissance: A History of Civilization in Italy from 1304–1576 A.D.* New York: Simon and Schuster, 1980.

Eby, Frederick and Charles Flinn Arrowood. *The Development of Modern Education*. New York: Prentice Hall, 1934.

Grenz, Stanley J. *A Primer on Postmodernism*. Grand Rapids, Michigan: Erdmans Publishing, 1996.

Harari, Yuval Noah, translated by Prottasha Prachurjo Sayed Fayej Ahmed. *Sapiens: A Brief History of Humankind*. London: Harvill Secker, 2014.

Haug, Werner and Phillipe Warner. *The Democratic Characteristics of Linguistic and Religious Groups in Switzerland*. Strasbourg, France: Council of Europe, 1999.

Herman, Arthur. *How the Scots Invented the Modern World: The True Story of How Western Europe's Poorest Nation Created Our World & Everything in It.* New York: Crown Publishers, 2001.

Hicks, Stephen R.C., *Explaining Postmodernism: Skepticism and Socialism from Rousseau to Foucault.* El Paso, Texas: Scholargy Publishing, 2004.

Isfeld, Dr. Sandy. "Shift … New Wine, New Wineskins"(Sermon, Airdrie Alliance Church, Airdrie, Alberta, September 17, 2006).

Jensen, De Lamar. *Reformation Europe: Age of Reform and Revolution.* Lexington, Massachusetts: D. C. Heath, 1981.

Jurgens, William A., translator. *The Faith of the Early Fathers.* Collegeville, MN: Liturgical Press, 1980.

Kienel, Paul. *A History of Christian School Education, Vol. I,* Colorado Springs: Association of Christian Schools International, 1998.

Kienel, Paul. *A History of Christian School Education, Vol. II,* Colorado Springs: Purposeful Design, 2005.

Kirby, Alan. The Death of Postmodernism and Beyond. *Psychology Now.* 2006. Issue 58.

Lessinger, Jack and Ranger Kidwell-Ross. *The Great Prosperity of 2020: Fall of "What's in it for Me?" and Rise of "What's in it for Us?".* Bow, Washington: SocioEconomics, 2009.

Markos, Louis A. *C.S. Lewis: An Apologist for Education.* Camp Hill, Pennsylvania: Classical Academic Press, 2015.

Mason, Roger A. and Martin S. Smith. *A Dialogue on the Law of Kingship among Scots: A Critical Edition and Translation of George Buchanan's De Iure Regni apud Scotos Dialogus.* Abingdon, England: Routledge Publishing, 2004.

McCrindle, Mark, Ashley Fell and Sam Buckerfield. *Generation Alpha: Understanding Our Children and Helping Them Thrive.* Sydney, Australia: Hachette, 2021.

McGoogan, Ken. *How the Scots Invented Canada.* Toronto: Harper Collins, 2010.

McKnight, Scott. *The Blue Parakeet: Rethinking How You Read the Bible.* Grand Rapids, Michigan: Zondervan Publishing, 2010.

Oliphint, K. Scott. *Thomas Aquinas.* Phillipsburg, New Jersey: P&R Publishing, 2017.

Pink, Daniel H. *A Whole New Mind: Why Right-Brainers Will Rule the Future.* New York: Penguin Group, 2005.

Sanneh, Lamin. *Translating the Message: The Missionary Impact on Culture.* Maryknoll, New York: Orbis Books, 2015,

Scofield, Cyrus I. *Scofield Reference Bible.* Oxford University Press, 1919.

Smith, Henry C. Christopher Dock: The Pious Schoolmaster of Skippack. *Christian Monitor,* January 1909.

Stark, Rodney. *Cities of God: The Real Story of How Christianity Became an Urban Movement and Conquered Rome.* New York: Harper Collins, 2007.

Stark, Rodney. *How the West Won: The Neglected Story of the Triumph of Modernity.* Wilmington, Delaware: Intercollegiate Studies Institute Books, 2013.

Stark, Rodney. *The Rise of Christianity: A Sociologist Reconsiders History.* San Francisco: Princeton University Press, 1996.

Stark, Rodney. *The Triumph of Christianity: How the Jesus Movement became the World's Largest Religion.* New York: Harper Collins, 2011.

Strange, W. A. *Children in the Early Church: Children in the Ancient World, the New Testament, and the Early Church.* Eugene, Oregon: Wipf and Stock, 1996.

*Switzerland Fertility and Family Survey 1994-1995.* Geneva: Federal Statistical Office (Switzerland), United Nations Economic Commission for Europe.

Tickle, Phyllis. *The Great Emergence: How Christianity Is Changing and Why.* Ada, Michigan: Baker Books, 2012.

Turley, Steve. *Classical vs Modern Education: A Vision from C.S. Lewis.* Scotts Valley, California: CreateSpace Independent Publishing, 2017.

Wagner, Tony. *The Global Achievement Gap: Why Even the Best Schools Don't Teach the New Survival Skills Our Children Need—and What We Can Do About It.* New York: Perseus Books, 2014.

Wiens, Delbert. *New Wineskins for Old Wine: A Study of the Mennonite Brethren Church.* Hillsboro, Kansas, 1965.